GEORGE AND ME
My Autobiography

GEORGE AND ME

My Autobiography

Angie Best

With Nicola Pittam

TED SMART

First published in Great Britain in 2001 by
Virgin Books Ltd
Thames Wharf Studios
Rainville Road
London W6 9HA

This edition produced for The Book People Ltd,
Hall Wood Avenue, Haydock, St Helens
WA11 9UL

A catalogue record for the book is available from the British Library.

ISBN 1 85227 022 5

Typeset by Phoenix Photosetting, Chatham, Kent
Printed and bound in Great Britain by
CPD, Wales

Contents

Acknowledgements

Thank you to my mum Mimi, to Dame Cicely Saunders of the hospice pioneer movement, to Paul Watson of the Sea Shepherd Marine Conservationists, to Page Hannah Adler for the Painted Turtle Camps for Chronically Ill Children and finally, thank you to my son Calum for allowing me to be a mum!

You can contact Angie at:

Best Bodys
PO Box 155
30765 Pacific Coast Highway
Malibu
CA 90265
USA

Email: bestbodys@aol.com

GEORGE AND ME
My Autobiography

Introduction

'George's footballing skills were a God-given gift; he didn't have to work at them. I think George would have been far happier and his life a lot calmer if he had found something more challenging to occupy his time, something he would have had to work at, something artistic or literary perhaps, something to push his limits and make him think. George has an amazing brain, but he was never given the opportunity to use it. In many ways it is sad that he was so gifted, that he didn't have to work very hard at being so good – because of that he got away with murder, absolute murder, God bless him.'

ON MORE THAN ONE OCCASION I have been asked why I didn't write this book sooner! Well, the truth is that initially I didn't want to write it at all, I suppose because I wanted to stay friends with George for our son Calum's sake. But now I can look at the situation in a different light and smile instead of cry! Calum is a grown man and has drawn his own conclusions. Everything that you are going to read has been written out of love not anger. It has also been written out of the realisation that whatever happens to us as individuals, whatever dramas we go through in life, they are our own doing. We have nobody to blame but ourselves. In short, we alone must accept responsibility for what we do.

Although George and I parted ways nineteen years ago, all anybody ever wants to ask me about is George Best. This was undeniably the case during my recent trip to London to promote my book on the menopause, *A Change for the Best* – nothing to do with men or football, but about women, and older women at that! Not so long ago George asked that I stop talking about him, so before the tour I asked my publishers, 'Can we try not to talk about George when I do my interviews for the book?' They in turn put in a request to all the newspapers that the questions be kept relevant to the subject of the book – the menopause.

Sure enough, first up for an interview was a young journalist who needed some material for an article. He of course had been briefed to keep to questions about the menopause, but he was soon professing ignorance about me and George because of his youth, and therefore had to ask me questions about that part of my life in order to get some 'background'. Now remember, I had been complying with George's wishes by asking journalists not to ask me questions about him. After all, he has a lovely new wife and our relationship ended nearly two decades ago; we have both moved on. Don't get me wrong: I would have been very happy to talk about George. I am eternally grateful to him for my wonderful son, an invaluable name and, as the youthful journo later put it, my 'leg-up into the headlines', but I also wished to observe George's wishes, so I refused to give the young man his 'background'.

When the article appeared, it was clear that he hadn't been best pleased with my decision not to talk about George, because he had peppered his piece with comments like 'How dare I not want to . . .' and 'Without George . . .', and that was just the beginning. After eleven days of some warm and sincere questions and some rude and impertinent ones, I had been badgered so much about George that I came to the realisation that this was a book whose time had come. It had to be written to allow George and Alex to get on with their lives without the ex-wife casting a shadow over them, and also to allow me to answer more important questions!

But it is one thing to write a book about women and the menopause, and a whole other ball-game to write a book about your life, even if you have kept diaries since the age of seventeen. George, of course, has published several books. I have not read all of them, although I have glanced through them and looked at the chapters about me just to make sure they were all kosher. I came across a few exaggerations, but I put them down to the old saying my journalist friend Nicola Pittam sometimes uses: 'Never let the truth get in the way of a good story!' So I started to come up with more justifiable reasons for writing my own account. And I found that there were quite a few.

One of those reasons was me. Our son, Calum, is now an independent twenty-year-old, and the connection that existed between George and me was severed a long time ago. George has a new wife, Alex, and I felt it was time for me, as they say in America, to have closure. It was time for me to write about George as I remembered him: young, physical, vibrant, gorgeous, intelligent, and a major pain in the arse. He was like a wild stallion, impossible to tame. I read all my diaries again for this book, and now that it's finished, I feel I've achieved that closure – with the man, with the relationship, with who I was and what I did (not to mention closure from cheeky young interviewers looking to use my past to prove their skills).

This means I can now move forward and start again, having forgiven myself and George (although I cannot be too much of an angel as there are some people who at times shared the path with us whom I feel unable to forgive). I always used to say, 'George has a lot to answer for.' It was many years before I felt I could actually begin to trust a man again. I would push men away if they started to get too close. As it turned out this was not necessarily a negative thing because it allowed me to devote my time to raising Calum, who now has his own life. I am starting the next chapter of mine.

When I started to read my diaries, I was hoping I would think, 'It's a little love story, really.' But as I got deeper and deeper into them, I realised it was not. It was a bloody nightmare, a time full of pain, anger and distrust. There were not that many sweet, loving moments. George is not and has never been a tender or romantic person (sorry girls!); you have to take his hand and show him the way. Nowadays, when people learn of my association with George they nearly always say, 'Oh, what a shame!', and I originally wanted to call this book *What A Shame*. In one way the whole thing *was* a shame, because of what George did to himself, even though it was in many respects a journey George just had to take. But then, I have never and will never think of our time together as a mistake because I ended up with a beautiful son.

This is, to tell the truth, more a book about my role in George's life and the mistakes we both made than it is about my life full stop. When I left George, it was almost as if I had never known him, never had anything to do with him. He was completely indifferent to me and I felt the same towards him. It was always difficult to get any real emotions out of George, to get him to be intense or dramatic about anything. That is just the way he is. George is a tortured soul, and over the years I have felt tortured too, but unlike George I believe I have come out the other side a stronger person.

This is a true story, a very hard story, and the people in it are just plain ordinary folk. Except George, of course. After all the good things I've done in my life, after all the amazing people I've met, I still wonder what exactly it was about the charm of this little Irishman that made him more important than any of that. I keep marvelling at the power he seemed to have over everybody. George is an original. His good looks are all completely natural (the George I remember had perfect skin, perfect hair and perfect blue eyes; he did not even have to style his hair), he had a supreme gift for football and he has an abundance of charm and charisma – which he has passed on to his son, thank goodness. He has done more in one lifetime than most of us would do in twelve. He was receiving 10,000 fan-mail letters a week at his peak at Manchester United in the late 1960s and he owned three nightclubs – Slack Alice's, Oscar's and Blondes – and clothing boutiques. He had money, he had fame, and on top of that everybody loved him.

During those eventful eleven days of my book promotion, it was put to me that George and I were the Posh and Becks of the 1970s. That one is really hard for me to swallow, because I know that during my time with George I had little control over anything. George and I were in effect ruled by the powers that be. We ran away from photographers and newspaper interviews, whereas nowadays our more assured successors are in control of their every move, have their own hotlines to the papers and almost crave the publicity. On a more trivial note, David Beckham, who is a very good-looking man, is not quite as handsome as our George, and George in his time, I think, was more adored by football fans, more celebrated, his appearances more eagerly awaited – and I can't sing!

My mother always held the view that when George was in his prime, football in England was a working man's sport and the working man had very little in the way of pleasures. He did not go skiing or abroad for holidays, he did not have a boat or a flash car, he did not have the leisure options available nowadays. His greatest pleasure was a cigarette, a drink and a football match once a week. And that, my mother reckoned, was what made George so special to them. He took them away from their mundane lives, gave them a ninety-minute escape at the end of each week. And it was not just the men he captivated; he gave pleasure to the women too because he was so gorgeous to look at. Older women adored him and wanted to mother him, teenage girls were madly in love with him and the men idolised him, so he did something for the whole family.

I think I had only seen a couple of football games before I met George. One of my first boyfriends, Barry Riseman, had taken me to Highbury to see Arsenal play, and my dad once took me to watch Southend, but when I met George I would try to go to every match he played in. I wouldn't say the game bored me, but I was much happier on the sidelines taking pictures of this gifted man.

But he wasn't quite everything he wanted to be. George's footballing skills were a God-given gift; he didn't have to work at them. I think George would have been far happier and his life a lot calmer if he had found something more challenging to occupy his time, something he would have had to work at, something artistic or literary perhaps, something to push his limits and make him think. George has an amazing brain, but he was never given the opportunity to use it. In many ways it is sad that he was so gifted, that he didn't have to work very hard at being so good – because of that he got away with murder, absolute murder, God bless him. As it turned out, the job I had signed up for – caretaker to an alcoholic – I was not gifted at. I didn't want to do it, but it was my job and I had to work very hard at it.

And the football was a problem in another way. George doesn't have very many friends because he has always been, and is, wary about the people around him. Over the years he has met so many people more focused on being an associate of George Best the legendary footballer than on getting to know the man himself, sharing his great sense of humour and his quick wit. This, of course, has over the years made him sceptical of almost everyone who comes into his social circle. Sadly, none of them ever did really take the time to find out who George was as a person.

I don't like to think that I went wrong when I married George – and not just because of Calum – but I certainly didn't realise that a handful of years of marriage would last two decades. When I looked back on my marriage and my relationship with George with the help of the diaries, I realised that I had thought I was the only one going through all the dramas, the booze, the women, the tall stories, the hardships of bringing up a family with precious little support (emotional as well as financial: George, for instance, was not always forthcoming in terms of child support, so I used to make up the shortfall in the only way available to me – by obliging the papers to pay me every time they wanted a quote or a story about him). That is, until I started getting letters from other women in similar circumstances around the world. So I would also like this book to be one big encouraging letter to all those women out there who still need to find the strength to make necessary changes in their lives. Hopefully, too, my account of George's path in life will make those who need to, think, 'Maybe I do drink too much; I certainly can't remember much about what happened last night. Maybe I should cut back on my drinking; maybe I should spend more time with my wife and children.' And if this book helps just one person, then that's another good reason why I could never give it the title *What A Shame*.

But there's one reason for writing this book that stands

head and shoulders above all others. I feel that I know what George is going through at the moment, and that is some kind of emotional cleansing. Sobriety will bring with it recollections of all the 'situations' George got himself into over the years, and very few of those memories will be good ones, so he is now having to deal with the things that he did, his treatment of other people. As his brain sobers up some terrible memories will come flooding back, and that has got to be a horrible situation to deal with. The guilt, the embarrassment – to my mind it must be so very painful for him. So if I tell all the stories here from my point of view, in a way I feel that I am giving George absolution. And it's a good time for that. After nearly a year of sobriety, and new implants, a new George is beginning to emerge, a George that most of us (including me) have never known. It is going to be interesting to see who this new man is. My guess is he is going to be pretty amazing.

I love you George, I forgive you George, but mostly I hope that in the cold light of day you can forgive yourself.

Everyone has a story, and this is mine. Well, mine and George's.

1 The Lady and the Tramp

'After years of boozing, women and disappearing acts, I knew as a wife and mother that I had to put Calum and myself first. Before then, I'd always been drawn back to George again and again, I gave him chance after chance. I would constantly tell myself that he was not a bad man, that he would eventually come to his senses if someone loved him, took care of him and showed him stability and trust.'

ANY TIME A newspaper or magazine asks me for an interview, they always begin with the same question: 'When did you know it was over between you and George?' And I always answer it with the same story.

If you are going to be homeless, then sunny California is the place to be. But on this particular morning in February 1982 it was raining, so I felt very sorry for a scruffy, dishevelled tramp I saw staggering down the middle of the road as I drove my car to the doctor's. Then my sorrow turned to anger as I had to swerve to miss him and my one-year-old son next to me began to cry. Nevertheless, I pulled over to check that the tramp was all right. As I did so I glanced in my rear-view mirror, and my anger turned to horror as I realised that the down-and-out looking so lost, standing there in a tatty, soaking wet tracksuit, was my husband and one of the greatest footballers the world has ever known.

I had not seen him for over a week. George had been on one of his infamous boozy benders and had disappeared. He often did that, leaving Calum and me for days at a time. On these occasions I never had to worry about whose bed he was falling into or out of, because when George was on a bender not a lot happened in that department. He could not get his balls in the net, had trouble scoring – you could even say he had problems with his tackle. I only had to worry about other women when George disappeared sober, but that only happened once.

On that occasion he ended up with somebody who professed to know better, but the popular singer concerned obviously fell under George's spell too (actually, I think he probably started out drunk but ended up sober).

In the beginning I had longed to have 'the happy family life', to be the perfect wife with a storybook husband, and to start with that is how things panned out. I even taught myself how to cook. I bought one of those fancy cook books and made steak flambé, chicken pies with homemade flaky pastry, any number of delicious dinners. Sadly, they were always still on the table the next morning; sometimes Dallas, my dog, ate really well at night. As you can imagine, it wasn't long before I stopped trying to be the little homemaker. In fact, Calum will say that if it hadn't been for restaurant take-outs he would have starved to death. I came up with a new name for single, hard-working mums who cannot or will not cook: 'food procurer'.

George was not a home-loving man. Well, he liked to stay at other women's homes, but with a drink or two inside him he certainly did not love his own. He didn't really know what home was or what love was, he was just a poor drunk who would lose his way home at night. Yet I also feared George coming home because his guilt would fuel his anger, and because of the demon drink I would also be in for a bout of sickness on any part of the furniture or carpet. I remember once being advised by the Centre for Rehabilitation in northern California to leave the sick for him to clean up when he sobered up. Yeah, right! I know the people in these places mean well, but following their rules sometimes makes life for other members of the family pretty miserable. I did try to follow their advice, but I was very reluctant to make that part of his problem my problem.

Anyway, seeing him there in the middle of the road was the beginning of the end for me. I remember thinking sadly, 'If I give my time and energy to looking after this man, how can I look after my son? The new baby deserves me more than the old one does.' It was a very sad realisation for me because in my mind we had come so far and had accomplished so much, even though in themselves each step was a very small one. I still did not feel ready to give up on George, but I knew that from that moment on it could not any longer be about me trying to make things work. If the relationship was to survive, it was up to George. Unfortunately, it was always easier for him to make a complete change than to fix what was broken.

After years of boozing, women and disappearing acts, I knew as a wife and mother that I had to put Calum and myself first. Before then, I'd been drawn back to George again and again, I gave him chance after chance. I would constantly tell myself that he was not a bad man, that he would eventually come to his senses if someone loved him, took care of him and showed him stability and trust. All these things I did, and all these thoughts, allied to a foolishly forgiving nature, kept me going year after year, woman after woman, club sacking after club sacking, withdrawal interlude after withdrawal interlude, upheaval after upheaval. When I look back at all those years of the same behaviour, just in different places, what on earth was I thinking?

There was a fun side to being with George, though. Everyone knew who you were and wanted to be your friend. And this didn't just happen to me: my whole family was popular. My sister Lindy would get asked out all the time, just because she was George Best's sister-in-law. When Lindy lived and modelled in the Middle East, in Tehran, one entertainer there even announced that he was going to marry her just so he could be George Best's brother-in-law! Then there was the night when I was waiting for my sister at the bar in Morton's, a restaurant in Berkeley Square, London. I was talking to a very nice man who seemed to be chatting me up. When Lindy joined us, I introduced her and then introduced myself as Angie Best. When he realised I was married, the comedian Jim Davidson completely ignored me and fell deeply in love with Lindy. He would send limos to ferry her wherever she wanted to go and they had a very sweet but short relationship.

When I first met George, in 1971, he was the gorgeous, raven-haired, blue-eyed, charismatic Irish footballer who charmed everyone. He was a superstar who had captured the imagination and the hearts of an entire nation. George was the focus of a national frenzy every time he ran out on to the pitch. After he was labelled 'El Beatle', women flocked to football matches – something which had never happened before – and he became a heart-throb. George was the first footballer to be pinned up on girls' bedroom walls across the country, and he soon built up a following as large as any pop star. To this day women tell me how much they hated me when they read about our engagement and marriage, about how they ripped down their posters of George when they read about us. I was disliked by his peers, male and female, because in their eyes I was taking their George away from them.

His influence was enormous. Any player who has even been compared to George will more than tell you that George Best is a critical and important part of where that player is today – not just financially, but by helping to create the stage upon which that player plays and by making it acceptable to play with flair as well as to do crazy things at times and get away with it. George was not only the first superstar player, he was the first to throw mud at the referee, the first to wear his shirt out of his shorts, the first to get sent off a number of times, the first not to show up at a game. The superstar players today get quite a bit more leeway in the game because of the things George did three decades earlier. Nobody knew what to do with him then, and nobody knows what to do with him now, but at least managers these days know more about how to deal with these shenanigans because they have learned a lot from the life and career of George Best.

George was a real man's man. Anyone who wanted to play in the game or who had aspirations of becoming a top-flight footballer was in complete admiration of him. George could do everything. He could play beautifully with both feet, he could tackle, he could head the ball, he could dribble, he could shoot. He was almost like a slalom skier with the ball at his feet. During training in his time with the San Jose Earthquakes in 1980/81, they would play a game called three on three. They would have the two goals about thirty yards apart and there would be three players against three players and a goalie at each end. The idea was dreamed up by Rinus Michels (who coached the Dutch World Cup teams for 1974 and 1978 and who invented the 'total football' philosophy at Ajax in the late 1960s) as a way of playing a fast, skilful game of marking and losing your marker within a confined area. George usually sided with Chris Dangerfield (my sister Lindy's husband) and another guy called Mike Hunter, and would often make bets with Chris as they walked out on to the pitch. 'I bet you twenty dollars that I can get their three players plus the goalkeeper sitting on their backsides before I score' – that type of thing. And he would do it, and Chris would be twenty dollars worse off. His ability to do things like that was amazing. No one else could even come close to that sort of brilliance.

In the late 1960s and early 1970s, the game was still at a stage in its history where the players would go out after a game to parties or bars, and all the girls would be there waiting for George. He was a tremendously good-looking guy and everybody wanted to be around him, the men as much as the women. He was entertaining and gracious to talk to. It quickly got to the stage where the other guys on the team would be talking to girls and telling them, 'Look, if you dance with me or let me buy you a drink, I'll introduce you to George Best.' Which really didn't help George at all.

I was eighteen when I first laid eyes on him, and I can honestly say that at that age I didn't really understand what all the fuss was about. I was modelling at a fashion show at Earl's Court in London for a company called Crochetta, owned by a man called Jonathon Hertz. That was my job at the time – I was a model. I had started out as a seventeen-year-old fresh from college in September 1969 as a personal secretary to George Walker, brother of Billy Walker the boxer; my friend Eddie Simon, who now runs the Allied Entertainment film company, got me the job. On my first day, I sat at my little desk feeling like a fish out of water, and I remember going into George Walker's office and pretending to do shorthand while he dictated a letter. I was, of course, supposed to type up the letter afterwards, but I just could not read my scribblings, and would never be able to read them, even though I had just spent a year at college learning how to. I still do not know how that happened. I think they were all very happy when I didn't come back the next day. I then had a brief stint as a receptionist for Vidal Sassoon, but I soon realised it was my looks that were going to enable me to earn a living.

So that's why I was modelling sweaters at a fashion show in Earl's Court. George was making a personal appearance there to promote his clothing boutiques. The show was dragging on a bit, then all of a sudden there was a commotion at a stand in the exhibition hall. People were craning their necks to get a better look, and then everything went quiet. I couldn't see a thing through the crowds and, intrigued, thought to myself, 'Oooh, I wonder what's going on?' Then the crowds parted and this rather short man with bad posture came walking towards me, everyone milling around him and making a fuss. No one was taking any notice of me any more – which was something that happened constantly when you were with George, no matter how beautiful you are or what you are wearing. I remember feeling quite indignant at this man stealing the limelight – getting on my high horse over such things was the Scottish coming out in me – and thinking, 'Well, I'm not going to make a fuss over him like everybody else is.'

So I didn't. But he did. Right in front of everybody he singled me out, first by sending over his minder to tell me that George Best wanted to meet me. I was absolutely mortified, and I wasn't having any of it. I quickly told the minder just that, which prompted George to come over himself. Even then the alarm bells should have started ringing: it was the middle of the afternoon and he was already quite tipsy (he later told me that he had been well and truly sozzled when he first spoke to me). But George soon turned on the Irish charm and had me laughing and hanging off his every word. He then totally shocked me by asking me to fly to Manchester with him that night. I was a mere teenager at the time, and I'd only just met this man. I was terrified at the thought of getting on a plane with a man I hardly knew, no matter how famous, good-looking or charming he was (Jonathon Hertz distinctly rolled his eyes when I went to tell him what had been said).

When the show finished I went to the airport with George in his limousine. By the time we got in the car he was well and truly sloshed, mainly because every time he had stopped off at a stand someone had given him a drink – although reasons weren't anything George ever needed when it came to alcohol. Excuses maybe, but not reasons. So by the end of the day George was, as they say, several sheets to the wind. I'd had enough. I was not going anywhere with this little drunken Irishman. George's response was to declare his undying love for me, ask me for my phone number and promise to call me the minute he landed. I gave him my number before I left, but of course I wasn't expecting to hear from him again.

True to George's form I never did receive that call, although my then room-mates, Angela Morris and Caroline Hayes, got excited every time the phone rang for about a week after, and we did follow his antics in the gossip columns. But it would be nearly five years and five thousand miles before our paths would cross again, and during that time I lived my life to the full. I had my own life in America, and a wonderful one at that, before I once again fell under the wild Irish charms of the one and only George Best.

2 A Model Citizen

'I had a really wonderful life for a few years in a beautiful area of New York with all the trappings of a rich, fashionable lifestyle. Allen and I lived in a lovely old building on the East Side. I'll never forget the first time I clapped eyes on his bedroom there – my first impression of how eccentric he was. The whole room, walls and ceilings, was covered in white fur. It reminded me of an igloo (and when I moved in it didn't take me long to change it).'

I WAS BORN ANGELA MCDONALD JANES to an English father and a Scottish mother (this is my true name, although I've been accused of adding the McDonald as an affectation when I lived in New York to make it sound more glamorous). I came into the world in July 1952 (to clear up yet another misconception, I have never lied about my age!) and my childhood was like any other youngster's growing up in the 1950s and 1960s in Southend on Sea, although it probably helped me a lot that I was a pretty child who soon learnt the value of a beaming smile. My greatest love, from the age of seven, was ballet. I never realised my ambition to be a ballet dancer but the classes I attended at the Eve Lincoln School of Ballet in Southend started me on the path my life would follow.

After my disastrously brief stint as George Walker's secretary and as a receptionist, my mother sent me to the Lucy Clayton School of Modelling, where I was immediately asked to join the books as a model. A photographer called Eric Swain took some pictures of me – I still love them – and he introduced me to John Mein of the Petal Model Agency. In no time at all my career was off and running, and so was I. I worked constantly, made what at that time was a lot of money and spent a lot of it at my favourite clothes store, Biba. I went out every night to Tramp or a gay club in Kensington. Angela Morris, whose nickname was Moll Doll, Caroline Hayes, who at the time was running the Vidal Sassoon School of Hairdressing, and

I would regularly dance the night away at these places. For a trio of good-looking women, it was best to go to gay clubs because you could dance your heart out and nobody would bother you.

My work in these early years included a shoot for the Pirelli calendar (I never actually got to see the finished article), a session with David Bailey, who took a picture of me with a tree growing out of the top of my head for *Vogue* magazine, and a trip with a model called Shakira, who later became Mrs Michael Caine. But my worst experience came in June 1971 when the German magazine *Stern* asked me to do a front cover with the then leading nude model, the gorgeous Vivian Neeves. She and I had a great time posing for their cover, and there was quite a difference in terms of physique: the lovely, curvaceous Vivian standing beside a pencil-thin me with no chest at that time. When the cover came out, to my horror, they had put her head on my body, her head on her body and said: 'Which looks best?' I was horrified but Vivian looked gorgeous - both ways!

But there were better experiences during my modelling career in the early 1970s. In September 1970 I was asked by Crochetta to go to New York and help them launch their new showroom there. I jumped at the chance. Within days of my plane landing in the States, I met a man who swept me off my feet, which I thought at the tender age of eighteen made everything complete (a rather naive notion I was slave to for a long time; only in the last few years have I come fully to realise that I can be a totally independent woman. I think women of my generation are betwixt and between. We can still hear our mothers saying 'You have to find yourself a husband', but on the other hand we are living our lives now in the midst of a new generation of women who are free-thinking in every way.)

Allen Bruce Schwartz had a famous clothing company in New York called Esprit, with a showroom next to Crochetta (nowadays Allen owns ABS Clothing, which puts copies of Oscar night dresses into the high-street shop window within days of the glitzy Hollywood ceremony going out live on TV). My job on that trip was to model the sweaters for the buyers who came in. Allen would come into the showroom on a daily basis and flirt with me constantly, and being the great salesman and genuinely nice man that he was, it did not take him long to sell himself to me. I went back home to Southend as scheduled a month later, but only to pack my bags and tell my mother that I was moving to the Big Apple.

Allen adored me, could not do enough for me; his words and actions were never less than highly flattering. He showered me with presents and poured attention on me. As a result, my memories of New York are warm ones. I will never forget, in particular, the Clairemont Stables in Central Park, owned by a man by the name of Paul, where I would go in the afternoons to ride horses – mostly old nags, but I loved the experience nonetheless. One day, close to our first Christmas together, I told Allen I was going over to the stables and he said he would meet me over there. I was very excited by this because Allen had never ridden with me before, so I phoned Paul and told him to get another horse ready. When I arrived at the stables, Allen was already there chatting to Paul, and I noticed a beautiful brown gelding with a wreath around its neck being led down a horse-box ramp. I said to Paul, 'What a gorgeous horse! Whose is that?' I asked him this question because there were a few rather glamorous models who wintered their magnificent horses at the Clairemont. But before Paul could reply, Allen turned round and said, 'Yours – Merry Christmas!' Naturally, I was ecstatic. From then on Rough Diamond (that was his name) went pretty much everywhere with me. I used to love to ride him on the beach during the summer at our house in the exclusive resort of West Hampton.

One of the things I remember so clearly, because it was such a novelty, is the fact that I had charge accounts in all the stores in my neighbourhood: butcher's, florist's, dry cleaner's, everywhere. I also had one at the department store Bloomingdales, but I didn't like to make use of it there because to my mind at a place like that I would be buying things for me, not stuff for 'us'. Still, having a charge account was such a new experience for me that I would go to the butcher and buy steak and other cuts of meat even though I had no idea how to cook them, just so I could walk out without paying. It was the same with the florist: our apartment was always full of flowers.

I had a really wonderful life for a few years in a beautiful area of New York with all the trappings of a rich, fashionable lifestyle. Allen and I lived in a lovely old building on the East Side. I'll never forget the first time I clapped eyes on his bedroom there – my first impression of how eccentric he was. The whole room, walls and ceilings, was covered in white fur. It reminded me of an igloo (and when I moved in it didn't take me long to change it). Thankfully, Allen had a lovely maid who would cook for him. I used to sit in the kitchen watching her, trying to absorb some of her know-how, but sad to say none of her culinary skills rubbed off on me (I once decided to try to bake a cake, but after the seventh try I'd burnt the baking tin so badly I had to throw it out).

The building was the same one where John Lennon lived with Mai Pang when he had split from Yoko Ono for a while. I found myself in the lift with Lennon one day and he started to lecture me about the fur coat I was wearing (well, it was the early 1970s and eco-friendly ways of living hadn't really got through to the public yet). I hadn't a clue how to react to this sort of talk, and I couldn't get away from him fast enough! Not so with my other famous neighbour, Greta Garbo, whom I used to see when I walked my Yorkshire terriers, Willy and Lulu, whom she loved. I had no idea who she was until Allen pointed her out to me one day. I was completely clueless when it came to famous people. Celebrities have never fazed me; to me they are just the same as everyone else (as my mother used to say, 'We all sit on the toilet the same way, darling'). I just thought this ageing Hollywood legend was a sweet old lady who never really spoke to anyone except me and my dogs. Just like Garbo, I loved my dogs. I also had a Dobermann called Mac (my modelling name at Petal) and a German

Shepherd I rescued from the pound in New York called Phaedra.

Allen continued to shower me with gifts. He gave me a stunning Rolls-Royce Corniche for my twenty-first birthday, which I thought was the funniest thing as I hadn't the faintest idea how to drive at that time (I gave it back and asked for a beach buggy instead). He also gave me a beautiful five-carat diamond ring – which I also gave back because it seemed to me that every woman wore one of those. The present I enjoyed the most actually came with the car. Allen invited me to sit on the front seat of the Rolls-Royce, and I soon realised I was in fact sitting on a gorgeous beige soft-leather bag from Bloomingdales. Inside the bag was a matching wallet, and secreted within opposite compartments of the wallet were a pair of Cartier diamond earrings and a matching diamond necklace, both of which my mother wears to this day.

Sadly, though, something was missing. It is wonderful to receive gifts, but deep down I did not really care for all these material possessions. I loved Allen dearly, but not enough, I realised, to want to spend the rest of my life with him. I felt this growing need for space, palm trees and blue skies. New York had been a fantastic experience and in many ways was the first step encouraging me to strive to be independent. Allen was very understanding about my feelings. Naturally he was hurt, but he wanted me to be happy and realised that I just had to go. So off I went on yet another adventure. I found very good homes for all my doggies. In fact, I left everything behind except for Rough Diamond, and I spent all my money on shipping him to his new home at Griffith Park in Los Angeles.

From a lavish lifestyle with everything anyone could ever want at my fingertips, I soon found myself in a room in the Beverly Hills Hotel with hardly a cent to my name, no job and no friends. But no 21-year-old could have been happier. As fate would have it, while I was staying at the hotel I met another girl I knew from the tennis club at West Hampton (that was another of my loves during that period of my life, playing tennis). Rhonda Young was doing exactly the same thing as me: relocating. She was a casting agent, and has since gone on to become a very successful one. Our brief relationship was to become a springboard for me into the next chapter of my life.

3 A Cher of the Action

'Then, just as Cher was about to sell me to the lowest bidder (as it were), along came my knight in shining armour – or should I say my footballer in a broken-down old banger. Into my life for the second time crashed George Best, and once more the social and emotional whirlwind whipped up and moved off. And off I went, caught up in the middle of it, to begin the Best and in many ways the worst chapter of my life.'

HERE I WAS in Los Angeles in April 1974, staying at the prestigious Beverly Hills Hotel with absolutely no idea of how I was going to pay the bill – or any other bill in fact. I had never had to worry about anything like that before, in my time with my parents or with Allen, and I had not yet learnt how to be financially responsible. Truth is, I never really have. I am pretty much clueless when it comes to money, partly because I have never felt attached to material possessions (an attitude that really helped me when, in later years, all my possessions were stolen not once but twice). Allen very kindly stepped in and paid the bill and gave me some money so that I could move into an apartment with Rhonda.

Everything seemed to be falling into place very quickly for me, as things have tended to do throughout my life. Rhonda took me to a casting for the *Donny and Marie Osmond Show* organised by Sid and Marty Croft, and I landed a role in a skit as Susan, Donny's date, who was snooty towards him but swooned over him when he was not looking. That was my one and only foray into the world of television, largely because Rhonda didn't have much of an opportunity to get me any other roles since I wasn't around for long.

Apart from Rhonda, I was still pretty much without friends in Los Angeles, but I was able to draw on some contacts I had made a few years back. When I lived in London, my favourite place to go was Tramp, the nightclub owned by Johnny Gold and Oscar Lerman. Oscar, who was married to Jackie Collins but has since passed away, made a big impression on me. He was a very strong, silent man, and although I didn't know him very well I felt a sympathetic connection. All the R&F (that's 'rich and famous') went to Tramp, and I became good friends with an American called Patrick Curtis. He took me out to dinner one night in a restaurant on the King's Road (our friendship was purely platonic as he was married to Raquel Welch at the time), and we ate at a table full of Americans. I remember being very nervous when I first got there, not knowing what to say to these people, all of whom knew each other, but it wasn't long before I got chatty, and then I realised that the man sitting across the table from me – a very handsome, tanned, slim and dark-haired American – was staring at me. When I finally made eye contact with him, he quite obviously mouthed the words 'I love you'; by the end of the evening, Mr Sun Tan himself, George Hamilton, had given me his phone number and told me to look him up if I ever went to Los Angeles.

Patrick had also done the same, if for slightly different reasons. 'Looking up' George Hamilton turned out to be a disaster – I felt he had little respect for me, and I was not about to be treated like a Hollywood bimbo, although after that first meeting we soon became good friends – but seeing Patrick again was wonderful. The social roundabout started spinning immediately: the very night I called him, Patrick took me to a party where I met Josephine Collins, another English girl, with whom I have now been friends for over 25 years. At the time, Josephine was managing the Gucci store on Rodeo Drive, and she invited me out to lunch the next day at a nearby restaurant. She took me to a little place eccentrically called Roughage and the Anatomy Asylum, owned and managed by a crazy little man called Richard Simmons, who was very outrageous, and still is (only now he is rich and very outrageous).

Richard had a large space at the back of his restaurant where he taught exercise classes, and he needed a teacher.

I confidently informed him that I could take over the classes, even though I'd only known the poor man for ten minutes. It all happened so quickly. One minute I was sitting in the restaurant talking to Richard, the next day I began teaching a class at the back of his restaurant. I lived at the top of Doheny Drive in Beverly Hills which was literally a hop, skip and a jump from the restaurant, so I walked to work every morning (I still did not know how to drive and I still had not learnt that walking was something no one did in Los Angeles). Soon I was overseeing five classes a day and being paid fifty dollars a week, including all the healthy salad I could eat. It seemed to me, and probably was at the time, the ideal job. I did it perfectly happily for about a year, and it never once occurred to me that I wasn't making much money.

I had no idea who any of the women in my classes were, sweating away in their tiny little leotards, until Richard took me aside one day and informed me that half of Hollywood was paying me to make them look good – stars such as Britt Ekland, Maud Adams and Priscilla Presley, to name but a few. One morning in the spring of 1975, this beautiful, very skinny woman walked in with her best friend. It was Cher and her pal, Paulette. Cher was actually pregnant with her son Elijah at the time, but you would never have known. They became regulars at my class. Cher worked very hard and loved to exercise, but Paulette preferred the social aspect to the classes. Needless to say, I had no idea who this exotic-looking beauty was until Richard, once again, came to the rescue and told me her name. But by then I had already used her as an example to the class, much to her chagrin, and I had also given her a perhaps unfortunate nickname – 'Bony', because I thought she had very beautiful bone structure in her face, shoulders, neck and hips.

Cher was doing her own TV show at this time (coincidentally directed by Art Fisher, who had overseen my role as Susan on the Osmonds' show) and one day she asked me for privately arranged classes so that she could fit them more easily into her schedule. I was more than happy to oblige her, as she was such a pleasure to teach. We had so much fun together over the next few weeks that during a hiatus in her TV show in June she asked me to go to Hawaii with her as her personal assistant. I'm sure Cher was not used to people turning her down, but I told her that I had no idea how to do such a job. Then she admitted that what she really wanted was for me to work out with her every day. 'That we *can* do!' I replied. Once again things were off and running, and the next thing I knew I was saying goodbye to a disgruntled Richard, had packed a bag and was off to paradise with a pregnant woman I barely knew, if the truth be told. It was not very responsible of me, especially as I left no instructions for the care of my horse in Griffith Park. (I later found out that the man at the stables had sold Rough Diamond and all my gear, and I immediately regretted my impulsiveness. Cher tried to buy him back for me, but the man said it was too late and he could do nothing about it.)

Hawaii was very beautiful and hugely exciting. We stayed at a fabulous house next to the Kahala Hilton and had little to do except exercise and sunbathe, eat and sleep, and during those lazy weeks Cher introduced me to needlepoint, which has been a passion of mine ever since. It felt like heaven on earth, until one day Cher decided she was going to go into premature labour. There I was in a strange land with a big Hollywood star who was six months pregnant and about to give birth horribly early, with no knowledge of how to drive a car, let alone find a hospital – I was in a total panic! I ran next door in a complete tizzy and the neighbour called a doctor who came over to the house and shipped Cher off to hospital.

But that wasn't the end of the drama. At the hospital absolute chaos reigned. Cher was on a drip to relax her uterus and physically could not speak to anybody. When people began to ring asking after her, I had no idea who they were. The phone in Cher's room rang constantly, there were doctors and nurses swarming all over her, and there was me frozen in the middle of everything not knowing what to do. And to make matters worse, Cher announced she wouldn't be speaking to anyone because she was so upset. Then Greg Allman, the father of Elijah, called and insisted on coming to visit her; suddenly, Greg was the only person on the planet Cher would speak to or see, which gave me a big headache as she had already refused, through me, to speak to her sister Georgeanne, her best friend Paulette, her manager Billy Sammeth, ex-husband Sonny Bono and Joe D'Carlo, her minder. So now everyone hated this 'new girl', suspecting that I had some hidden agenda because I barred them from speaking to Cher, when all that was really happening was that I had just got my head stuck up my rear end wondering what on earth I was doing.

Poor Bony looked so helpless and fragile lying in her hospital bed. But Greg was coming to see her so she asked me to wash her hair. Well, just imagine: 26 years ago in a hospital in Hawaii. It was not exactly Harley Street, let me tell you. The hospital had no modern conveniences whatsoever, but Cher kept asking me: 'Angie, will you wash my hair and make me look nice for Greg?' So there was I with this beautiful long black hair in a bucket, washing and rinsing, backwards and forwards to the sink for clean warm water. Anyone looking in on the scene would have found it hilarious. Somehow I managed to get her looking clean and beautiful for Greg's visit.

When Greg arrived at the hospital, he immediately offered to stay with Cher at her bedside, letting me go home after hours of madness. Unfortunately, when she saw him all her machines went off the charts and she started to contract. The doctors and nurses got very nervous and told me to tell Greg that he couldn't stay. So now *he* hated me as well! After more hours filled with explanations and Cher promising to stay calm and Greg promising not to upset her in any way, I finally got to go back to the house on the beach.

At that time I was seeing Desi Arnaz Jr, the son of Desi Arnaz and Lucille Ball. He was a lovely boy, despite spending most of his time on another planet; having said that, I just thought he was a very spiritual human being who was fascinating to be around. Desi chose this moment to arrive in Hawaii, which created more problems for me, even though I was delighted to see him. You see, in Hollywood at that time everyone was so generous and open; whatever they had, you could share. It was a different culture. I came from England, where people were not generous in the same way, probably because most of them didn't have as much to share. When I was growing up in Essex, if somebody wanted to come and stay in your house permission was usually sought first. But this was Hollywood (albeit in Hawaii), and Desi just showed up on the doorstep. I was mortified because I thought Cher would be furious if I let him stay. I of course eventually found out that she loved the idea, but at the time I had no idea that it was OK for things like this to happen.

I remember being scared stiff at the thought of telling her about Desi staying at the house, but I kept thinking that I had to because eventually she was going to come home from the hospital and there was going to be an uninvited male guest in her house.

So I went to the hospital and anxiously blurted out in front of Greg: 'Oh, Desi showed up at the house. I think he's come to see you.' Which of course made Greg angry until Cher explained with more tact that he was there to see me. It all seems so ridiculous now, but at the time I was just too embarrassed to tell her he was there to see me, because you just didn't do things like that back home! I felt terrible, but Cher loved the idea of Desi coming out to see me, saying, 'Oh great, you've got some company.' And I remember feeling a bit silly afterwards and thinking, 'God, that was easy.'

It was a cultural thing, perfectly normal for Californians however unnerving it was for me. I recall a similar thing happening in November 1984, when my sister Lindy had her baby and I was dating the actor Val Kilmer. I had gone to her house while she was in the hospital having her son Nicholas, and one day Val showed up on the doorstep. It was a much easier moment to handle because of my experiences in Hawaii and subsequently, but it still threw me because he just arrived unannounced. He slept on the floor that night. Can you imagine: Val Kilmer, sleeping on the floor. Mind you, he was not a famous actor back then.

Cher was soon back from the hospital after the false alarm, and all her family and close friends came to visit. Then, in August, it was time to pack up and get off back to Los Angeles and work commitments. We went straight to Cher's enormous house next to Engelbert Humperdinck's, off Sunset Boulevard. I was, needless to say, having a fabulous time working for Cher, meeting some very interesting people from the movie and music business along the way. In fact, that had been the case ever since I arrived in LA.

I have already mentioned the fact that I got in touch with George Hamilton when I first arrived in Los Angeles. Despite those unpromising beginnings, as I said, we soon became good friends and one evening in the summer of 1974 he and Sammy Davis Jr took me to Las Vegas to see the King, Elvis Presley. After the show, we went backstage and Elvis's manager, Colonel Tom Parker, came over to me and said, 'Mr Presley would like to meet you.' George Hamilton was having none of that, and declined, but when he was off having a chat with someone else, leaving me alone at the bar, the Colonel came over again and this time I said yes. So off I went into Elvis Presley's dressing-room all by myself. Well, he was lovely. He told me I was the most beautiful girl in the audience – a comment he reserved just for me, I'm sure! He asked me about my home in England and what brought me to America, and we indulged in all kinds of small talk. He revealed to me that he was very unhappy and very miserable at that time in his life. Then he pulled a turquoise ring off his finger and gave it to me, wrote down several phone numbers in my little black book and made me promise to call him after we said our goodbyes.

Now I had no intention of ever calling the King – he was a lovely man, but I didn't really go for his type – but it was made impossible for me anyway because, as I learned from my friend Josephine fifteen years later, George

Hamilton told her that he had changed some of the digits in my phone book to make sure I could never call him. I have to say, though, that the ring Elvis Presley gave me is still a treasured possession.

Perhaps understandably, my relationship with George Hamilton did not last long. Despite that, I continued to live an idyllic life, even running off to the rodeo once with the actor James Caan, but things were starting to get a little difficult for me. Cher did not really need a trainer at that point in her life, principally because she was now a full-time mother with a little baby, so as the summer of 1975 turned into autumn I found myself having to play the personal assistant role instead, and I didn't know how to go about it. I made one mistake after another simply through not knowing about the business – for example, Cher would get a call from an important songwriter and I would take a message when I should have patched the songwriter straight through – and there was no one around to point me in the right direction, tell me where I was going wrong. Cher was used to having things done properly, and when they were not she got irritated, and that irritated me.

Then, just as she was about to sell me to the lowest bidder (as it were), along came my knight in shining armour – or should I say my footballer in a broken-down old banger. Into my life for the second time crashed George Best, and once more the social and emotional whirlwind whipped up and moved off. And off I went, caught up in the middle of it, to begin the Best and in many ways the worst chapter of my life.

4 Georgie Porgie, Pudding and Pie

'There was no doubt that he was attracted to me, and I was attracted to him too, so I sat down at the bar and began to chat to George. It was, in effect, our very first date. We both felt that pull of attraction as we spoke, but I should have read the warning signs much more clearly than I did.'

If someone had said to me thirty years ago that I was going to marry a footballer, let alone George Best, one of the most famous practitioners of the art in the world, and have a son with him, I would have laughed at them. Indeed, such thoughts were the last thing on my mind when in October 1975 I was invited to a Beverly Hills party in his honour.

I got a call from a guy called Ed Peters, a Beverly Hills socialite who threw a lot of parties. He told me he was having a soirée for a British guy called George Best, and because I was English he thought I would like to come. I thought to myself, 'Oh, I met him once. Yeah, I'll go.' So I called one of my girlfriends, Colleen Camp, an up-and-coming actress who later married Peter Goldwyn of the Goldwyn Studios, and asked her if she would come with me. So Colleen and I went off to this 'soirée', but it was a nightmare from the minute we walked in: in the house there were about five men – one of whom was, of course, George – and about fifty women. It was dreadful. I introduced myself to Ed, thanked him for the invitation, went up to George and said, 'Nice to meet you again, I met you once before, blah, blah,' and left. I just could not get out of there quick enough, to tell you the truth, especially as George was not on his best form that night – actually, I remember him looking like a scruffy little herbert. Colleen and I went off to one of the trendy social clubs in Los Angeles and left the Irishman behind with his beer.

After that experience I didn't give the man another thought, although obviously I'd been in George's mind because a few weeks later I got another call from Ed. 'George is having a party at his bar and he would like you to come,' he said, adding that he would pick me up and drive me to George's bar in Hermosa Beach and then drive me home. Now I've never been one to turn down a party invitation, and despite the off-putting nature of the last party Ed had invited me to, I agreed to go. Ed picked me up at Cher's house as promised and drove me to Bestie's, but when we got there it was apparent there was no party going on. It was just George's little way of getting to see me.

There was no doubt that he was attracted to me, and I was attracted to him too, so I sat down at the bar and began to chat to George. It was, in effect, our very first date. We both felt that pull of attraction as we spoke, but I should have read the warning signs much more clearly than I did. Despite the fact that it was only the third time I'd ever met George, I'd already seen him drunk and scruffy, and now, as we chatted at the bar in Bestie's, a young girl came straight up to him and kicked him. I honestly did not know what was going on. I was completely naive when it came to this kind of behaviour. The girl's actions took me completely by surprise; I had never seen behaviour like that before and I had never dealt with any kind of jealous woman (although I would soon learn how to). I remember looking at George and thinking, 'Oh my, the poor thing', but I didn't say anything or make a fuss because that was just not the way I went about things. So I kept quiet as George disappeared into the back room of the pub to argue with this girl, who was in a bit of a state. If I had got into a tizzy like that in the coming years every time I saw George with a new girl, I wouldn't have had any fingernails left.

I had little idea about his playboy reputation at that time. I had been living in America for several years so I didn't have a clue how George's life had panned out since I'd first bumped into him at that Earl's Court fashion show. I hadn't read a British newspaper since I'd been in

America, so I had no idea how notorious his behaviour had become. To be honest, all I saw were those beautiful blue eyes, the little dimple in his chin and the cheeky look about him, and I sensed an amazing chemistry between us. I also sensed that George was an original, a real-life character, and that was exciting. There have been few of these 'originals' in the public eye – Oliver Reed, Michael Caine, Richard Harris and Richard Burton spring to mind – but these wonderful people were, and in some cases are, real personalities, and attractive because of that. Nevertheless, I walked out on George on that 'first date', and Ed Peters took me back to Cher's house.

It is too easy with the benefit of hindsight to say what I should have done or should have known. I should have realised a stable relationship would be a problem with such a man when that young girl stormed into the bar and tore a strip off him in front of me. I also should have heard the alarm bells that ring when you meet a man who likes to hang out in bars. I had always been the first to criticise English women for being with men who lived down the pub, yet here was I contemplating doing exactly the same thing – wanting a man whose first home would never be the house he shared with his partner.

But physical and emotional attraction plays with your powers of reasoning; there are times in our lives when we girls just don't act sensibly. I left Bestie's that night once more expecting never to hear from George again, but a few days later I got another call asking me on another date, and I agreed to see him. After all, I couldn't really say that George had done anything wrong that night in the bar; we were having a great time until that girl came in, and George was only trying to contain the situation by taking her off like that. So George drove up to Cher's house in Beverly Hills on this occasion, but when he arrived he didn't know how to get in. He didn't know that he was supposed to ring the buzzer and announce his presence, so he ended up staying outside the house for ages trying to figure out a way of getting in. It was hysterical, although of course it hadn't helped that he was drunk. Now I do not mean this offensively in any way, but George comes from a very down-to-earth, relatively speaking simple background in Belfast and he looked and felt totally lost and uncomfortable standing there in Cher's Beverly Hills mansion. Then we got into a bit of an argument over some small matter and George, fuelled by the drink, behaved in what I thought was a very ungentlemanly way. On our first date he'd had a row with another girl and on the second he was drunk and pretty much unmanageable. Not a good start in anybody's book.

Of course the sensible side of me was saying, 'OK Ange, you can see the signs now, don't let it go any further.' But I was powerfully attracted to him and I genuinely enjoyed his company. At the time George and I first began to see each other, I was very naive and saw George's wonderful and charming nature (as anyone who has met George knows, he can charm the birds out of the trees) and his good looks before I saw the negative aspects to his character. He was completely different from the American men I had been dating. We slept together on our fourth date when I went to a pool lunch at Ed Peters' house. Of course George, being a man, has put it on record that we had sex on our first date, but that is not true. I had always been a bit prissy when it came to promiscuity (at the time I was known in Beverly Hills as the Golden Box, a dreadful expression which meant that I did not sleep around as was fashionable then), but I have to admit that my attitude was totally different with George. I'm sure all the girls reading this will know what I'm talking about if they have ever fallen in love. It's just different. It feels right.

After that first time together it seemed as though we were in each other's pockets twenty-four hours a day. The relationship blossomed; it was like an addiction for both of us. Several times I went down to Hermosa Beach to see him, and several times he came up to see me in Beverly Hills. But even at that early stage, he carried on displaying his other side. It is said that love is blind, and how right that is. One night when I was with him I said, 'I've got to go, George. Cher's got an important appointment tomorrow and I have to be there.' George kept insisting that I spend the night with him, but I was adamant and went to get in my car. But I wasn't going anywhere that night: the tyres were completely flat – they had nails in them. George denied responsibility for this over and over again, but much later, when he was drunk, I did get him to admit what he had done that night. If there's one good thing that comes out of men getting drunk, it's the fact that they are more likely to tell you the truth.

Despite these little episodes – and boy, there were plenty of them – on a practical level George came into my life at the right time. I was ready to leave Cher's place and I think she was more than ready for me to move out as well. So once more, in the early spring of 1976, I packed up my few belongings, this time with the intention of moving in with George down at the beach. Needless to say, perhaps, things were a nightmare from the beginning, with one little drama after another, day in, day out. George was a very quiet, unassuming man really, but drama seemed to follow him wherever he went. We often, for instance, had girls coming up to us in the bar and accusing George of making them pregnant. Every week, it seemed, there was another young girl who was supposedly bearing his child. They would even show up at the house while we were both sitting there watching TV, and cause a commotion. How could one man get into so many pickles? But he did! These girls could not have cared less if I opened the door; they were determined to have their say, and they did.

I remember when I first got together with George there was one particular girl who had known him during his days in Manchester. She wrote just the one letter, its subject her pregnancy. I asked George what he wanted to do about it and, true to form, he did nothing, hoping that if he ignored her she would just go away. And she did. Indeed, no one has ever come forward to claim that they are raising one of George's love children, which to me is a huge surprise. The number of women George has slept with is staggering, and to think that none of these liaisons has produced a child is mind-boggling. And I'm sure if one of these girls had had a baby, they would have come forward. There has been ample opportunity for them to stand up and make a claim, but not one of them ever has.

George has said before that he moved to America to get away from being constantly recognised and harassed like this, but it was still a problem for him, although not as bad as it had been in England. George would often, for example, get weird letters from men and women in prison. There was the woman who said she knew when George was trying to get in touch with her because she got messages from him through the lyrics of certain songs played on the radio. Then there was the man who was convinced that George visited him in his cell. He knew when George had paid him a visit because certain parts of his anatomy would bleed. There were hundreds of letters like this, some so unbelievably deranged that I kept them for years until eventually they went into the bin, during one of my periodic attempts to clear all the emotional and physical debris out of my mind and house.

I remember another day in 1979, in London at a pub called the Pheasantry, which is a perfect example of the sort of harassment George had to put up with. My sister Lindy and I were going out with George for dinner. We had just ordered some wine for us and a vodka for George at the bar when a man came up and kicked him in the ankle for no reason at all. George just turned to us and said, 'Come on, let's move away.' He didn't want any trouble, so we all moved to the other side of the bar, but this man came with us and proceeded to kick George in the ankle again. Well, I was just flabbergasted. The man then started baiting George: 'Come on, George Best, what are you going to do? Hit me? Do you want to put my name in the papers?' To his credit, George carried on ignoring him, but I felt terrible about it. It put such a dampener on our evening. It made me feel incredibly sad whenever I witnessed people antagonising him for no reason. Most of the time he just shrugged these incidents off, but as he became more and more dependent on alcohol, he tended to lose his temper more easily and would give them the satisfaction of retaliating. But then, who should have to put up with goading like that?

A similar incident occurred the next year when my sister's boyfriend (now husband) and George's former San Jose Earthquakes team-mate Chris Dangerfield went out for a 'quiet' drink with him. George's usual post-match routine in San Jose would be to go into a local pub and play darts. On one of these occasions Chris walked into the pub in front of George, and George was immediately confronted by a West Ham fan who asked, 'George, would you sign an autograph for me?' George replied, 'Sure, I'd love to,' and took the napkin that had been thrust in front of him, signed it and handed it back to the man. Only the guy was not satisfied with just that one autograph. 'George,' he continued, 'would you mind signing one to a friend of mine too as he told me that his daughter came up to you once and asked you for an autograph and you told her to f..k off.' George calmly said, 'No mate, I wouldn't have done that. Thanks very much,' and started to walk away. But the man stood in front of him again. 'I'll tell you what, George. Why don't you write on this piece of paper "I never told your daughter to do that" and sign it George?' So George, still trying to avoid trouble, said, 'I'll be more than happy to give you another autograph, mate, but that's it.' George and Chris again made to walk away, at which point the man took a swing at George. Fortunately, he missed; unfortunately, his fist managed to connect with Chris. And this incident was just the tip of an iceberg in terms of what George would have to go through with men no matter where we were, whether it be Los Angeles, London, Manchester or Spain.

On the other hand, George loved it when girls threw themselves at him. Even though to American women he was not a huge celebrity, just a home-town Hermosa Beach one, the number of girls fluttering around him on the beach was incredible. Most people in America had never heard of George Best, but these girls loved him because he was an original and he was just being himself. That is the George that everyone always falls in love with, including me: the man with the sense of humour, the twinkle in his eye and the Irish charm.

We lived right on the beach in those early days of our relationship, and everywhere we went girls would scream 'George, George, we love you!' right in front of me. Most of them had no shame at all, and we're not just talking ditzy beach girls here wanting to mother and smother him in love; this sort of behaviour was echoed by middle-class City girls in London too. I remember one night when George came home completely drunk, so much so that when I opened the front door for him he staggered straight into the bathroom and passed out over the toilet bowl. This was at about three in the morning, but suddenly there was another knock at the door. I opened it and the poor woman standing on my doorstep almost passed out herself with shock. 'I – I just wanted to check on George,' she stammered. 'Here he is,' I replied, throwing open the bathroom door and revealing George in all his glory, draped over the toilet. She turned on her heels and fled without a word. And in the poshest of restaurants women would not think twice about dropping into George's lap matchboxes with phone numbers scribbled on the flap as they walked past our table where we would be having a quiet dinner together. These poor girls thought that if they left their number on a matchbox, or on a piece of paper under the windscreen wiper of his car, he would actually call them!

And there was no escape from this sort of behaviour. It was just as bad when I went to watch George play football on a Saturday afternoon. I would be sitting in the stands at the San Jose Earthquakes ground, surrounded by all these girls screaming at George, despite the fact that he never took any notice of it while he was on the pitch. I sometimes think they yelled like that simply because I was there; certainly, if George missed a chance they would stand up and say something like, 'George, you're not scoring like you did last night!' before giggling and looking in my direction. I used to have to put up with things like that everywhere I went, so it wasn't only George who felt harassed by fame. There was just no getting away from it.

In fact, it was terrible what I went through. The only time I had any peace was when I was at Cher's, or out with Josephine in Beverly Hills.

And there were other patterns of behaviour I had to start coping with right from the very start, like George's love of treating a pub as his home. My sister Lindy came to visit us on the beach one night and we went out looking for George, because that is all we ever seemed to do: traipse around bars trying to find him. The search would often just go on and on. If a pub crawl failed to track him down, we'd go and look on the beach in case he'd passed out on the sand, which was another favourite pastime of his. Well, this particular night we didn't get as far as the beach because we found him propped up in a bar not far from Bestie's. Lindy and I ended up staying and having a drink with him, even though I was desperately trying to get him to come home because he was pie-eyed.

There was a girl sitting on the opposite side of the bar. I had not even noticed her, but Lindy had because this girl was flirting quite outrageously with George. Lindy pointed her out to me and it took me a few moments to realise what she was doing. She was sitting at the bar playing seductively with her drink and giving George a real look; George was lapping it all up. I think she was as drunk as he was, because I just could not believe she was being so brazen when I was standing just a few feet away from him. I would never have done that to another woman's man.

Well, this went on for about ten or fifteen minutes, and George was so drunk he was just smiling straight back at her. I couldn't summon up the confidence to confront the girl, but finally she got up off her stool and went to the bathroom. While she was gone, Lindy told the barman to pour the girl a glass of iced water and tell her it was from George. She then wrote a little note on a napkin and sent it over with the drink. I watched fascinated as this girl got back to her stool, saw the drink and napkin, looked over at George, flicked her hair, smiled at him again and read the note. Then her face dropped and she went a deep shade of red, picked up her bag and left the bar. Of course, I was howling with laughter along with Lindy, and it was only then that she told me what she had written on the napkin: 'Hi, I've noticed you've been watching me all night. I've sent over this drink so that you can pour it on your crotch and cool off. Love George.' George also thought it was hilarious when I told him what Lindy had done, but there was no danger of the episode driving home a point with him. The little trick worked that night as it helped us to get George out of the bar, but it certainly did not stop him from picking up women in the future. Indeed, the very next night he was back at the pub enjoying the same experience all over again.

But of all George's less endearing qualities – and don't forget, there were many that were highly attractive – it was his drinking that would drive me crazy. I think one of the reasons he reached for the bottle so often was because he had a desperate need to be one of the boys. When George first blazed a trail through the footballing world, there was no one to coach him on how to handle all the attention he was receiving. When he got into trouble on, and especially off, the pitch, he found he was on his own. Nowadays they make football personalities, they design them and they dress them; they have managers and publicity agents to help them cope with life in the spotlight, but George was the original who paved the way for all this. He *was* a team player, but because he was who he was, he found it very difficult to *be* a team player. He could never be just ordinary.

Partly because of this need of his to be ordinary, to be wanted and loved, I soon thought of a couple of nicknames for George. I always needed to have some way of getting across that feeling of one-on-one attention that George loved so much, some kind of familiarity that was just about me and George, because all the football boys called him Bestie and everyone else referred to him as George. My first nickname for him was Mushy, after the mushy peas he liked to eat – a very Manchester thing, I think. I had never heard of them or seen them before, but George insisted on a can of mushy peas with every meal – well, the meals he actually ate. Then I began calling him His Lordship, which he loved.

Despite all my efforts, though, George was incorrigible – although to what extent I hadn't yet figured out. As I said, the night after Lindy's clear message to that girl at the bar, His Lordship was back there perched on his stool enjoying two of the three things that mattered most to him in life: a drink and a woman. His other love, of course, was football, and that was starting to suffer seriously as well.

5 Poetry in Motion

'I tried to be the perfect girlfriend and wife over the years, sitting waiting at home for him every night. His happiness meant my happiness in those days, and I did everything I could to make life at home as easy and as welcoming as possible. I even learnt how to cook – a first and a last for me.'

FOOTBALL WAS GEORGE'S life, and when he played for Manchester United he lived and breathed the game. When he moved to America and started playing there, he did not seem to care so much, although he still had the occasional flash of brilliance on the pitch. It was in 1980 during his stint with the San Jose Earthquakes that George scored what he considers to be the best goal of his career. In one of his own books he admits that period of his life was not a good one because he was drinking too much and had been plagued by injuries to his right knee. But that afternoon he showed his genius once more. After being kicked and tripped up by an opposing player, George took the free-kick himself, then got the ball back, adamant the other team's players were not going to touch it. He set off and wormed his way through five of them before putting the ball in the back of the net. George has said of that goal, 'I didn't know how I did it then, and I still don't. When I see it on television it still dazzles me.' But at this stage of his career the dazzling moments were few and far between. It was no longer important to George if he missed training, or even a match. In fact, when he joined the San Jose Earthquakes, he missed the press conference to announce his transfer to the squad because he was on a bender.

When I began dating George in 1975 his respect for the game was still intact. It was just a few months before he was approached by Fulham with an offer to play for them during the 1976/77 English soccer season, a deal which still allowed him to travel to the United States to play for the Los Angeles Aztecs during the summer months. At that time many big stars were playing in the American league, like Pele (who was with the New York Cosmos team), Johann Cruyff and Franz Beckenbauer. George would still go out drinking, but he never missed a match at this time and could still turn on the fancy footwork, even with a raging hangover. He often ran rings around the other guys on the pitch without trying or getting out of breath. Because he could still do that with so little effort, he slowly began to spend less and less time practising and more and more time in the bar, usually only showing up at the team ground on a Saturday for the match itself. I would go to watch him at the home games, and I would feel so proud of him when he ran out on to the pitch. More to the point, for an hour and a half on a Saturday afternoon I could be sure where George was and what he was doing, and for me that was a big relief, even though I knew that straight after the game he would be back in the bar with the boys.

We lived in our little house on the beach when George was playing during the summer of 1976, and I adored the place, but I was so relieved when it was time for George to go back to England to play for Fulham. I loved living in Los Angeles, but I was sick to the back teeth of all the daily dramas, the merry-go-round of booze and women that George just could not seem to get off. Don't get me wrong: at this point in our relationship he was still the charming little Irishman who had swept me off my feet. George may have rolled in at 4 a.m. with his pocket full of other women's phone numbers, but the next morning he would be so wonderful to me that I would feel like the only woman in his world. He was never one for showing affection or being terribly romantic, but let's face it, George had a tough upbringing on the Cregagh council estate in Belfast in the 1940s with his parents, three sisters and one brother.

Even nowadays George does not really feel the need to

keep in close contact with his family. Neither did His Lordship ever really talk much about them. The first time I had any contact with them was January 1978 when he called them to tell them we were getting married. I spoke to his mum, Ann, on the phone and she sounded lovely. When he told her about our engagement she said – in contrast to my mother, who was very sceptical about the match – that she was very happy for us, although I'm sure she'd heard it all before. But later that year Ann passed away, and her funeral in October was the first time I actually met any of George's family. His father, Dickie, is a lovely man. They are all very down-to-earth, sweet folk, and you can tell they are a close family even though they don't keep in touch very much. The whole family have a sort of veneer of reserve, but behind that there's an understanding that they love one another and would do anything for one another. They just don't feel the need to express it, that's all.

I think George was too young at the age of fifteen to go off to Manchester United; I think he should have been made to finish school. Dickie has received quite a bit of criticism over the years for allowing his son to leave school and cross the Irish Sea on his own at that tender age, but I don't think Dickie should be criticised for not going with George. Once the decision was made and Manchester United had given their assurances, there was no point in both of them, father and son, being overwhelmed (in the sense that everything would have been so different to what they were used to) by a trip to England. Anyway, George knew that his parents were proud of him, just like I am of our son Calum. I celebrate Calum every day, I cannot bask enough in the glow of him, just like my mother with me. She was so proud of me and told everyone, including me, how she felt. I try to savour every moment with Calum, although he hates it when I make a fuss. George is not a big fuss-maker either. I remember once getting very enthusiastic over something we were going to do and I was being quite exuberant when His Lordship just turned to me and said, 'Stop it, be quiet.' It really hurt my feelings and I have never forgotten how unnecessary that comment was, but then George was never taught how to express his feelings and obviously found it embarrassing when others did so in his presence. Such emotions came more naturally to him in the early stages of drunkenness. Then he'd have his little moments when he would tell me that he loved me, but only after a couple of vodkas. Being impulsively romantic did not come naturally to His Lordship.

There were drinkers in George's family – although I didn't find out that his mother also drank until her funeral – but it's hard to judge whether or not the urge to drink is hereditary. George was devastated when his mother died. Although the coroner recorded a verdict of death by natural causes, George in a way felt terribly guilty and blamed himself. You see, Ann had started drinking later on in life, when George became famous, and he thought he was the cause because she could not handle his fame. Unlike George, who drank anywhere and in any bar, Ann would drink at home behind closed doors. When she died, George went into a terrible depression, berating himself for not being there more often for her. But I think that even if he had been in Ireland instead of five thousand miles away in California he still would not have been able to reach out to her. He was the same with everyone else, and there's no reason to think it would have been any different with Ann.

When he was drunk, George could go either way – nastiness and meanness, or flirtation – but when he was sober he was quiet and withdrawn. George built walls around himself all the time. Even though we were married and I was the person who knew him best, he never really gave me the same intimacy and affection I gave him. I would have laid bare my soul for him had he asked me to, but I know he would have had trouble doing that. He kept things to himself. If he had a problem, rather than come home and talk about it he would go off somewhere and let off steam by having a drink.

And he didn't just do this with me; he never really

became close to anyone. His former team-mate (and my sister Lindy's husband) Chris Dangerfield, despite not spending all that much time with him, considered George a good friend, but he too admits that he never got really close to him. It was difficult for His Lordship or anyone else to break down those barriers he put up. He'd been pulled in all sorts of different directions throughout his life and career, so the withdrawal was very much in self-defence. It was hard for him to give himself to any one person at any given time.

Knowing all this, when George did little things for me it meant the world, like the time when, just after he'd left on a two-week trip to play a series of football matches, I went into the bathroom to find a note on the cabinet saying 'I love you.' And another in the fridge. And another in my underwear drawer, stuck to a pair of knickers. A fourth note revealed itself when I pulled back the bed sheets that evening. This was one of the occasions I can recall when George showed real romantic affection towards me, and because it was so rare it made me feel really good. Every now and then he would also surprise me with a poem he'd written, or a piece of prose about his life in Belfast. I have kept all of these precious items, but George won't let me share some of them with you.

One love poem he wrote for me in 1979, with the title 'For My Wife', is absolutely beautiful. I wish I could have reproduced it here for you to read. George also wrote eloquently and intensely about very personal matters, the pain he felt, and his drinking. As well as writing these wonderfully evocative poems, George would sometimes sit down and write great stories about his Belfast childhood for me to read. I loved them. Often the stories were unfinished. I'm sure he always intended to come back to them, but they were just one of the many things in George's life that got lost along the way. George is a good writer; it's such a shame he has never been encouraged by his peers to explore these different avenues. It is these times, these treasured possessions I look back on now whenever I think of George. So often in his life he has been a caricature of what he once was. To me, George will always be the loveable charmer.

I tried to be the perfect girlfriend and wife over the years, sitting waiting at home for him every night. His happiness meant my happiness in those days, and I did everything I could to make life at home as easy and as welcoming as possible. I even learned how to cook – a first and a last for me. I would spend hours every night slaving over a hot stove. My culinary skills were soon the envy of all our friends. After a while it became obvious that this was just pointless, and I got fed up with it and stopped cooking for him. Even now I don't frequent the kitchen. It is just not something I want to do any more.

I never complained when he came home drunk. I knew even then that it was pointless to yell and scream at George; he just would not take any notice. Of course there were times when I did have a good moan, but he would just turn round and walk straight back out of the door. More often than not, though, His Lordship would just come home, throw up and pass out on the couch or on the bed. If he'd been on a particularly bad binge he could get nasty, and at those times I would try to avoid him as much as possible. I did everything I could to accommodate His Lordship and his needs, but I was too idealistic when I was young. I used to think constantly of all the ways I could tame him and curb his drinking: hiding my purse so that he couldn't get even more money, putting sleeping pills in his tea in the vain hope that come the evening he'd be snoozing like a baby instead of going out on another bender, arranging things for the two of us to do together. I was determined to attain the perfect relationship. Of course, now that I am older and wiser, I know that you can never stop someone else drinking. They have got to want to stop first.

As a slave to the drink, His Lordship by definition did everything he possibly could to thwart my dreams. I soon realised, for instance, that he was not happy unless I was sitting at home. As long as he knew where I was, that was OK, but he would get very jealous if I went out with my friends or if I spent time with Cher. So, again trying to accommodate his needs and emotions, I used to sit at home and build model cars to keep my mind occupied. I even built a model sailboat once, but I remember one night George getting angry at that for some reason. George tried to make the sailboat fly, and sure enough it flew straight out of the window! He was in so many ways like a little pouting boy who would get upset when things didn't go his way but, unlike a child, who would tend to sulk when upset, George would just reach for the nearest bottle. When he began drinking in one of those moods it was hard to keep out of his way; he would be looking for an argument. After a while I came to realise that one of the reasons he was trying to pick a fight with me was so that he would have an excuse to storm out of the house.

On occasions such as this, when I'd been out and George was at home working himself into a lather, I would come home and find all my belongings in the dustbin. Our place on Hermosa Beach had a rubbish chute that fed a big container underneath the building, and on several occasions I had to grab a torch and climb into that damp, dark container to fish out my possessions. In fact, it got to be something of a ritual. I would walk in and say, 'George, where's all my stuff?' And he would pout and huff and puff and say, 'I dunno,' when I knew he'd shoved everything down the chute, dirty and smashed up, just like the mood he was in. I'd climb into that container and find clothes, jewellery, pictures, toiletries (even my toothbrush) – anything and everything. When this first started happening, I took into account his state at the time and tried to soothe him. 'It's OK, honey, it's OK,' I would say. 'I love you. I wasn't doing anything, you can trust me, it's OK.' It was madness, really. I mean, what was he doing with his life except everything he was accusing me of doing? *He* was the one drinking, seeing other women and staying out for days at a time. There was always one set of rules for His Lordship and one set for everyone else.

That is one of the reasons why in August 1976 I was relieved to be going back with George to London and

Fulham. In my young, naive way I thought that if we were far away from the beach and all those tempting girls, George would knuckle down with his new club, behave himself, begin to act like a real boyfriend and pay me the attention I deserved. How wrong I was!

6 Revving Up for a Round

'I always had a pretty good idea of what he was getting up to as I'd catch a whiff of perfume or find the tell-tale scraps of paper with phone numbers on them when I emptied his trouser pockets. He never tried to hide these numbers when he was drunk. It was almost as if he was proud of them. When I asked him if he had been with a woman at her house or somewhere else, he would never deny it. We both knew where he had been and what he had been up to.'

DIFFERENT CLIMATE, DIFFERENT location, different people, but the same old George and the same old problems. I was so hopeful that once we got back to England and we were around people we knew and loved that George would feel encouraged to change his ways and become a person who better fitted the stereotype of a good partner that I held in my imagination.

As soon as we arrived we went straight to Michael Parkinson's house, who was, George had told me, a good friend of his. I suppose everybody had their preconceived ideas of what I would be like, and looking back on it now I suppose I seemed to be just another one of George's 'girls'. But, as young as I was, my relationship with George was very important to me, and I was very disappointed by Mary Parkinson's attitude towards me when I arrived at her house. I am sure she thought she was being hospitable, but I felt I got a cold reception. Michael wanted George to play in a charity cricket game for him, and afterwards George sat with Mary and signed hundreds of autographs. George was good publicity; Angela could have been abducted by aliens as far as anyone was concerned. Although I must say in Mary's defence that a few months later she did ask me to appear on her daytime television show, and I let her down.

There was, of course, a reason for my failing to show up. I didn't go because George had come home so late the night before the show that he wouldn't get up and go to training at Fulham. I was furious with him, but I just could not get him to get up. I was supposed to go to the Thames Television building, but I was so annoyed and upset with George that I couldn't go anywhere in the state I was in. Of course Mary was furious with me for not turning up, and quite justifiably too.

In my time with George I have several times been on the receiving end of the celebrity cold shoulder. I remember one incident in particular during those first months back in England, with the Scottish comedian Billy Connolly – a story my sister Lindy told me only recently when she found out I was writing this book. She once found herself riding in a limousine with Billy (and a few other people) and remembers Billy making a number of comments about me and my marriage to George that she found very hurtful. Lindy has told me that, with steam coming out of her ears, she leaned across, tapped Billy on the knee and introduced herself. Lindy told him about how much I'd done for George: how I was the one who had bought him clothes and paid for everything when I first met him, how I was the one who had taken him to the dentist when he hadn't been near one in fifteen years, how I'd looked after him, etc. Lindy reckons Billy was suitably chastened by this because a few days later, when he bumped into her in Tramp, he apologised for his behaviour in the limo.

Not long after this little scrape, we were all gathered together at the restaurant Morton's in anticipation of George's surprise appearance on *This Is Your Life*. My mother, my father, Lindy, everyone was there. Lindy and I were standing there chatting with our dad, Joseph, who was wearing a smart light grey suit and puffing away on a huge King Edward cigar. Then in walked Billy. He saw us straight away and, perhaps still feeling bad about that night in the limo, came right over, shouting, 'Och aye, how are ye?' Lindy introduced my dad to him, and Billy, in his eagerness, lunged forward to shake his hand, spilling a whole glass of red wine all over my dad's grey suit in the process. Dad was devastated and Lindy just let rip, telling

Billy that he was not scoring any points with our family. Billy again was very apologetic.

There were some nights during our time in London when George would stay at home with me and we would watch television together, and other nights when he would come home after just one or two drinks, but again, they were few and far between. At that time Tramp was *the* place to be seen in. All the hip and trendy people went there, so every time George finished a game with Fulham, whether they won or lost, he would leave Craven Cottage and head straight for Tramp. If I ever wanted to find him, Tramp was always the first place I looked. But because of the way he drank, he managed to annoy at one time or another just about everyone in there, getting into more and more fights and being barred from the place more times than I care to remember.

In those days, George didn't need a reason to get into a fight. When he was really drunk, it might only take something as silly as a draught when someone opened a door near him to send him off into a tailspin of rage. Any old excuse would do when he was in that sort of a mood. In his cockiness he thought he was Muhammad Ali, but no one would fight him because he was George Best. No one wanted to punch George, no matter how much he goaded them. Later in his drinking life, this state of affairs turned full circle, but back in the 1970s the guys still respected him as a player and would just say, 'George, you're drunk, I'm not fighting you,' and back off (although George, being George, would rarely let it end there). Today's generation doesn't know all that much about him, doesn't care about him as much. My generation loved him, and it was usually George looking for the fight; now it's younger lads looking to make a name for themselves, so that they can brag to their mates that they punched George Best.

I've already described several of these awful situations, and usually, in later life, George didn't rise to the bait, but Calum told me about an incident on one of his visits home to see his father recently. When Calum came to England, if he ever wanted to hang out with his dad he had to do it in his father's second home – the local pub. One night they were in there playing pool when a young Italian man put his money on the table to play the winner. He obviously followed that up by saying something to offend George, because George then whacked him with the pool cue and threw him out of the pub. Ten or fifteen minutes later, Calum was on the phone in the pub when he heard a terrible noise. He walked back round the corner and was confronted with a full-scale bar fight, in the middle of it all his father and one of George's crazy Irish friends, surrounded by a vanful of Italians who had come back to seek revenge. So Calum, who was just seventeen at the time but already six feet tall, instinctively threw himself into the mêlée to protect his dad. 'Dad and I were looking at each other,' Calum recalled, 'but I couldn't get to him because there were too many people, and the next I thing I knew I had been hit over the head with a bar stool.' That was a father-and-son bonding session George-style.

George is still an icon to people of a certain age, but to the younger generation he is just an old sot, a caricature of what he once was and the stories they have heard about his exploits on the pitch. And that is really sad, because George was in my opinion the greatest footballer this country has ever seen, but now he is more famous to a large section of the population for his drinking and womanising. You will never hear another footballer say a bad word about George – they all still have the greatest respect for him. Bobby Charlton, his former Manchester United team-mate, may say George 'could have done so much more', but he still acknowledges his amazing talent. Chris Dangerfield told me that no matter what happened with George and his drinking, every player he came across still wanted to play with him or against him. They all loved George's generosity on the pitch. He didn't show much of that in his personal life, but as a footballer he set the standards. He was possessed of the complete game, which meant that alongside every skill you could wish to have he had vision and helped other players reach their potential. A lot of players have aspirations to be like this, but George made it happen, almost effortlessly, and produced those magical football moments that everyone remembers.

George played at the top of his game throughout the world, and was respected wherever he went. When he was with the San Jose Earthquakes he would go, along with Chris, to training and it was the coach's habit to leave a pile of kit on the ground for the players; if you didn't get there in time, you'd have to go without. Apart from George. His stuff was always placed in the corner, clean and neatly folded, despite the fact that half the time he didn't even show up (on which occasions there was always a fight to wear George's kit). Things were so tight at San Jose that the players would have to insist in their contracts that they got transport to and from the ground. One guy called Timmy Shultz was given a push-bike, which became his way of getting around. Poor Chris got the team Volkswagen bus with the name 'Earthquakes' written down the side, but only on the understanding that he picked everyone up on the way to training. George was given a rental car.

This idolising of George the celebrity footballer had been on the wane in England ever since he left Manchester United for good in January 1974 and then spent some time in the United States. But now he was back at Fulham, George was becoming trendy again. People were starting to take notice of him once more. But there were downsides to this. It didn't help, for instance, that George was in the papers nearly every week, usually photos of him either leaving Tramp or being thrown out of Tramp. Soon, everyone knew he was back in town.

I rarely went to Tramp with him. However, there would be times when we would go out for dinner with some friends and then stop off there for a drink afterwards. Those times were usually fun, because George would just have one or two drinks and then come home with me. But on other occasions, especially if he went there on his own or with some of the boys from the team, he usually came home drunk, or not at all. When that happened, he would spend the rest of the next day sleeping off his hangover and would only get out of bed for fish and chips, a Chinese takeaway or to go to training. And then only if I threw a bucket of water over him.

I was stuck in this horrible flat in Park West, the flat Fulham Football Club had put us in, but it was so rotten and disgusting and crawling with cockroaches that I could not bear to touch anything. My mother had to come up from Southend to give me a hand to make it look more like a home, because I was crying my eyes out and just wanted to leave. I hated it so much. George just shrugged his shoulders and left me to get on with it. I so desperately wanted us to live like a normal happy couple, with a nice little home. I would go out to buy things for the flat to cheer it up, some furniture and little things to make it seem cosy and homely. But nothing I did made any real difference; the flat could never be a home while George was being his usual self. I was aching to leave and find somewhere of our own, but the football club insisted we stay, I suppose because they did not want to show favouritism to any player, and with all the players living in the same area they could better keep an eye on them. Little did they know that it would take more than a flat and four walls to keep an eye on His Lordship. We had been promised so many wonderful things by Fulham, but we were desperately disappointed. That is when things really started to go downhill.

After just a couple of months back in town, George started again on his binges. Up until then he had been pretty good. He would still come home drunk, but at least he was coming home at one or two in the morning after the pubs and clubs shut. Now he began to roll in at 4 a.m., then 6 a.m., and then he would go missing for the night. I always had a pretty good idea of what he was getting up to as I'd catch a whiff of perfume or find the tell-tale scraps of paper with phone numbers on them when I emptied his trouser pockets. He never tried to hide these numbers when he was drunk. It was almost as if he was proud of them. When I asked him if he had been with a woman at her house or somewhere else, he would never deny it. We both knew where he had been and what he had been up to.

And I always knew when a bender was underway because he would start to sleep later and later and he would stop shaving. And if I looked out of the window and saw George's car parked outside, it was confirmed. I know that sounds daft, but if George knew he was going to be on a binge for several days he never took his car with him. He knew the state he would get into, knew he would not be able to drive, and also knew that he would be able to go home more easily with whichever girl took his fancy that night. When that little routine started to take hold he would be lost to me for a week. I knew that the reason for this was that despite the bright new beginning offered by Fulham, George was getting more and more unhappy. He was feeling very let down by everybody and he felt nobody was fulfilling their commitments to him. All George cared about once more was being one of the boys and making the team a winning side. But the harder he tried to make that happen, the worse things seemed to get, and he began to seek solace in the bars every night. All too soon the bad days began to outnumber the good.

One Saturday late in October Fulham lost 5–2 to West Ham and we went to a restaurant called Alexander's on the King's Road with the boys for dinner. George was not in a very good mood and began to sink drink after drink. At half past one in the morning everyone was ready to go home – everyone except George, who decided he wanted to go to Tramp. He went round the group one by one asking everyone to go with him, but after a busy day all anyone wanted to do was go to bed. I too told George I didn't want to go to Tramp, and that was when he got really mad. He refused to come home with me and insisted he was going to go on his own. When he was in this kind of mood I knew better than to argue with him, so we both got into the car and because I was sober I drove him to the club. When we got there, he was still trying to get me to go in and have a few drinks with him, which was rare for George because he hardly ever drank hard in front of me. He preferred to go out on his own or with the boys, leaving me at home in front of the TV. But I was adamant. 'Please don't go in there, George. Come home with me.' But His Lordship, being the headstrong, stubborn man that he is, got out of the car and went in anyway.

My reaction to this? I drove our car straight into the back of a Rolls-Royce parked in front of me. To this day I don't know what possessed me to slam my foot down on the pedal. All I can say is that the despair and futility of trying to make George see sense just welled right up inside me. I was just sitting there in the car fuming as George disappeared inside, thinking, 'What can I do to make him come home with me?' I felt in that moment that I just had to do something to make a big impression on him, to prevent him from staying inside that nightclub, to come home with me instead of getting hopelessly drunk. And I just put two and two together, got five, and in a split-second had ploughed his new Jag right into a Roller. Both cars ended up as write-offs. I was not injured, but all the waiters came out of the club to find out what was going on, and everyone was milling around me and the cars on the street. Everyone except George. None of this had the slightest effect on him. When it was clear he was not going to emerge, I quite calmly got out of the Jag, got into a taxi and went home.

George was furious with me when he found out what I'd done, but at the time he could not have cared less. If I'd thought, even for a moment, that my little tizzy at the wheel of his Jag was going to make George listen to me, or make him think twice before he picked up another glass, I could not have been more wrong. He came home the next night as drunk as a skunk and started ranting and raving about the amount of money I had cost him. I just told him I didn't care, that the cost of fixing the Jag was nothing compared with all the money he had wasted on drink over the years. We argued on until George just turned on his heel and walked out. It really was a crunch time in our relationship. This time he stayed away for two days, but when he did eventually come home he begged me to give him another chance. Foolishly, I did.

You see, as big a problem as George's drinking was my

willingness to forgive him again and again. I loved him so much that he could have come home covered in blood and holding a butcher's knife, but the minute he looked at me with those eyes and asked for forgiveness, I would have melted.

7 Bunny Girl

'I was already doing some modelling during the day – mostly photo shoots for poster ads and the like – which kept my mind off George, but I still wanted something else to occupy my evenings with, and a job as one of the world-famous Bunny Girls at the Playboy Club tickled my fancy and seemed the perfect solution. I walked into the club to see the Bunny Mother, Serena Williams, and she hired me on the spot. I became Bunny Angela.'

ACTUALLY, I CONSIDER forgiveness to be one of my better traits. When I was with George I could quite easily have been hailed as the Patron Saint of Pardons. When George showed remorse for almost anything he did I would just say, 'That's OK,' and we would carry on our lives as before. It never once crossed my mind after rows or embarrassing incidents to leave him. In a way that was a good thing. I had been an independent woman most of my life, so when he went off on his benders, rather than spend fruitless hours waiting up for him I would just go to bed, knowing that George would turn up sooner or later like he always did. And during the day I would make arrangements to do my own thing.

Throughout that 1976/77 season at Fulham life fell into a certain pattern. George would behave himself for a few weeks and we would have a brief shot at normality, then he would be off again. When the miserable drinking spells began to last longer than the happy dry spells, I began to get fed up. George would profess his undying love for me every time he messed up, and I would accept that, but slowly I was beginning to realise that his words would never mean anything. One night when he didn't come home I found out he had spent it with a popular entertainer. I often wondered if these women knew about karma – what goes around comes around – because every one of them knew George and I were a couple. I would never dream of taking another girl's man, and naturally there were times when I just wanted to ask these girls why they did it. In fact, I did call the woman concerned to ask her if she'd seen George, and she said, 'Yes, he spent the weekend.' But she was just one of a long procession. It really didn't bother me as much as you might expect, because His Lordship always came back to me, but there was one occasion, late in 1980, when George tried to pick up another woman that absolutely horrified me. That woman was my sister, Lindy.

George and Lindy had always had a great relationship. My sister had lived with us on and off and was always there for me. So it came as a great shock when she eventually told me how my own husband had tried to hit on her. Thankfully, she didn't tell me about it until years later, when George and I were no longer together, because she was so embarrassed and did not want to hurt me. And then she only admitted it because I questioned her about him. You see, George had told me when he was drunk that he had hit on my sister. We were having one of our arguments at the time, as we sometimes did when His Lordship was several sheets to the wind, in a foul mood and trying to bait me by putting something between us to break up our closeness. He was trying to blame her for his actions, but on the day he was talking about, in San Jose, I had only sent her to the airport to pick him up because I was pregnant and did not feel well enough to drive.

Lindy had arrived at the airport on time, but she waited and waited for George, who was returning from an away game, as flight after flight came and went. His Lordship finally appeared, drunk as usual, and told Lindy that he needed a cup of coffee. She took him to the airport café, but then George changed his mind and said he needed the bathroom. Again Lindy waited and waited, until eventually she realised he had disappeared on her. After much searching, she finally spotted him leaving the airport and jumping into a cab, so Lindy got in my jeep and followed him to a bar called Hulahans. After confronting him there, she eventually got him to leave and drove him home. She pulled into the garage and was just about to get out of the jeep when George grabbed her arm. He was extremely drunk and began telling her how he wanted her and how all along she was the one and he had been in love with her and not me.

Lindy told me she just wanted to throw up when she heard all this – she had never seen the pitiful, disgusting side of His Lordship before. George had always been cheeky and playful around Lindy, never flirtatious or, as she described the way he was in the jeep, like a 'slimy snake'. She told him in no uncertain terms to pull himself together, got out of the jeep and came into the house. To this day I do not know how she did not tell me there and then, but I am grateful to her that she didn't. Lindy had adored George up to that point. She of course had seen him drunk before, and knew about his antics, but she also, like me, knew how lovely he could be when he was sober. But that incident completely changed her view of him, which was a terrible shame.

Well, as I was saying, come December 1976 I was fed up with George's behaviour. He was out at Tramp every single night and in the papers for the wrong reasons all the time. I was so furious with him and with Fulham for not keeping an eye on him that I demanded they give me my own flat. Can you believe I had the nerve to do that? I was adamant that I wanted to move out and away from George, but I couldn't afford anywhere on my own, so I told Fulham I wanted a flat of my own – and they gave me one. It was across the street from George so I still had to put up with his comings and goings, but at least I had my own space and was out of his way. I had pretty much had it with his shenanigans, with his treating our relationship so carelessly, and as soon as I moved out I decided to give His Lordship a little shock of his own – in more ways than one.

One night before Christmas, after George and I had just had yet another fight, I called a friend of mine, Lynne, and asked her to go out for a drink with me. I was sick of all the heavy dramas, sick of looking like a chump, and just wanted to have some lighthearted fun for a change. Well, that night Lynne introduced me to a West Ham football player called Billy Jennings. You would have thought that footballers would be at the bottom of my to-date list after George, but I took one look at Billy and thought he was the cutest little thing on the planet. So he filled up my time during this break from George. I never told George about Billy as I was too terrified of his reaction. I knew I had to tread very carefully. Billy was wonderful though, he understood my reasons for wanting total discretion, and he kept to his promise. Nonetheless, our so-called romance fizzled out within two months, but it wasn't Billy's fault. I was just too jumpy and never wanted to go out anywhere in case George or anyone else saw us.

Despite meeting Billy, however, just days later I was still feeling as though I wanted to give George a taste of his own medicine and assert my independence at the same time. One day, walking down Park Lane in London, a brilliant flash-bulb of an idea went off in my head and I turned round and headed straight for the Playboy Club. I was already doing some modelling during the day – mostly photo shoots for poster ads and the like – which kept my mind off George, but I still wanted something else to occupy my evenings with, and a job as one of the world-famous Bunny Girls at the Playboy Club tickled my fancy and seemed the perfect solution. I walked into the club to see the Bunny Mother, Serena Williams, and she hired me on the spot. I became Bunny Angela.

Serena was thrilled to have me on board, but none of the girls were. They made it clear that they took a dim view of me just walking in off the street and taking one of their jobs. They had all worked and trained hard to achieve their position, and all of a sudden there I was, taking all the publicity, but Serena loved it and the spotlight on her club that came with it. She even organised a press conference. I hadn't realised it was going to be that big a deal; I thought it was going to be just a couple of reporters. But being the Scot that I am I stuck my nose in the air and said things like 'George is not going to walk all over me!' My comments made the cover of every single newspaper. I cringe now when I remember those headlines, like I'LL BE

NOBODY'S DOORMAT!, but I'm so glad that I did it. At the time it was all so much fun, so hysterical. It was just the best (excuse the pun).

As a result, I was also able to get out of the flat Fulham had given me and move into my own. But despite my life being so busy, I realised I was very lonely, especially at the Playboy Club because none of the girls wanted to become friends with me. In fact, they all hated me, which I suppose was an understandable reaction in some ways. I was given the plum job of casino receptionist, which meant I did not really have to do anything. I couldn't anyway because I wasn't trained; I never, for instance, learned how to do the Bunny dip. So I would get there on my own, get dressed on my own, do the work on my own and then go home on my own. It was tough at the time, but now I just look back and giggle at how marvellous it all was, to have had the power to do that kind of thing, even though I was only at the club for a short time.

Of course it took George all of two seconds to find out I was working at the Playboy Club after my face was splashed all over the papers. He came into the club one night and I thought he was going to cause some trouble because he was so drunk. He had been wearing the same clothes for three days. But all he did was lose all his money gambling on the tables and stagger off home to pass out. Whenever I saw George like this, in such a desperate way, I always had the feeling it was his way of reaching out to me and asking for help, so after work I went round to the flat to check that he was OK, but he was dead to the world. I managed to get him undressed, and found the usual scraps of paper in his pocket, which I tossed on to the already considerable pile on his coffee table. Had he wanted to, George could easily have made an in-depth study of why women like to scribble down their phone numbers!

Now that I was working during the day and in the evenings and living my life away from George, His Lordship began to get possessive again. He had said in the past that he loved my independence, that it was 'like a breath of clean, fresh air', but that was a long way from the truth of the matter. He could never handle it if I looked at another man, let alone spoke to them.

An awful example of this happened one night in February 1977, when George tried to strangle a friend of mine in Tramp with his bare hands. I had gone out for dinner with a lovely couple, Ann and Lawrence Ronson. I had just made friends with them, and they were the nicest people you could ever wish to meet. After dinner at Alexander's, we decided to go to Tramp for a few drinks. Of course George was in there, drunk as usual, and from the minute we arrived he got it into his head that I was with Lawrence, which was completely untrue. But there was no telling George in his state, and seeing me in the company of this other man was like a red rag to a bull. All of a sudden, George attacked poor Lawrence, grabbing him by the throat right there and then in front of everyone. Ann and I were mortified, but could do nothing except look on in horror as the bouncers dragged George away from Lawrence, who luckily was not hurt badly. Needless to say, we quickly left. The Ronsons went straight home and I went back to my flat. I felt so sorry for them. What had started out as a nice evening having dinner with new friends had turned into an utter fiasco.

The next day I saw His Lordship coming up the road towards my flat. I immediately locked all the doors because from the look on his face I could tell he was not in the greatest of moods. In fact, he was fuming, and it didn't take him long to kick down the door and come storming through. He found me cowering in the kitchen. I tried to calm him down by telling him that Lawrence was only a friend, but George's brain was so mixed up that he wasn't about to listen to me, and after punching and kicking his way through the door he turned his attentions on me. He left me lying on the kitchen floor, I presume to go to some pub because I know he didn't go home. The next day he was so nice to me, no one would have believed that a matter of hours earlier he had been acting like a raging monster.

George was a completely different person when he went on a binge. He could be so mean with the demon drink inside him, but when he sobered up he was always pleasant, full of humour and, well, frankly irresistible. He desperately needed help to control the Mr Hyde side to his character, brought on by the drinking, but he didn't seek that for a few more years. I soon came to realise that he was not the only one that needed help. I did too. I was tired of all the drunken outbursts and knew that I had to teach myself to give His Lordship up, no matter how much I loved him, no matter how wonderful he was when the drink hadn't taken hold of him.

I was ready to return to Los Angeles. I had made up my mind to leave George for good. I carried on working at the Playboy Club so I could get the money together to buy a plane ticket back to America, but then fate stepped in and offered me a way out – although not before George did something that confirmed to me (if in fact I needed further proof) that what I was doing was unquestionably the right thing.

I was working in the club one night late that February when I got a call saying that George was in hospital. I steeled myself not to react; I was absolutely determined not to go rushing off to his bedside. Calmly, I checked with St Stephen's Hospital in Chelsea, where he had been taken, and they told me that he was indeed injured but not seriously. Having got that information, I decided to go home and get a good night's sleep. It turned out that the night before had been one of the rare occasions on which George had taken his car out with him. He had become so drunk that he had crashed it into a lamp-post outside Harrods department store on the Brompton Road. He was on his way home from Tramp at the time. The police on the scene said that George was too ill to take a breathalyser test; the doctors added that in a way it was lucky that he was so sozzled because he was so limber from the effects of all the alcohol that when the car smashed into the post his body, instead of instinctively stiffening, just went with the momentum. According to one police officer, 'The facial injuries indicate he struck the windscreen sharply, or his head went through it.' If George had had time to brace himself, his injuries could have been much worse. As it was, His Lordship had to have stitches in his head and he had fractured his shoulder and collar bone.

The press, of course, had a field day with the story. Naturally, they rang me looking for some comments and I just gave them the usual spiel of how worried I was and that I hoped this would make him think twice before drinking and driving again. But deep down I knew George would be lying in his hospital bed desperate for a drink. I went to see him at the hospital the morning after the accident, and he looked awful. There were stitches all over his head and his hair was matted together with blood. But it wasn't so much the sight of George that made me catch my breath. No, it was the little soccer groupie who was in the room with him. Without being too crass, let's just say she was preparing to 'do a Monica' on George. I just threw the pair of them a disgusted look and left.

I never went back to the hospital, and George didn't call me while he was there, but several days later when he was released the first place he came to was the Playboy Club. I was shocked to see him as it was obvious he had come straight from his hospital bed. He hadn't even been home to change, because he had on the clothes he had been wearing when the accident happened and they were covered in blood. His hair was still slightly matted too, and it looked as if he hadn't shaved for days. Luckily, Serena and the club were very understanding and let him in, but all he wanted to do of course was drink and gamble. He never once came over to talk to me, but I could see him watching me out of the corner of my eye. When he'd lost all his money, he stumbled out of the door and went home.

Not for the first time, I was furious with him for turning up at my place of work in that state, and I swore to myself there and then that I would book my flight back to LA that weekend. George was just never going to change. The most important thing to him was not having a loving family or a stable home or even a long-lasting monogamous relationship, it was all about where the next drink was coming from. I was desperate to leave, and someone up there must have been watching over me because at work the next night, which was Friday, 6 March, Serena came over and said that there was a phone call for me. Half expecting it to be His Lordship, I picked up the receiver and was shocked to find Cher on the other end of the line. She asked me to go back to Los Angeles to work with her and get her ready for an upcoming tour. I did not need to be asked twice. I agreed immediately, and she booked my flight.

That weekend, I told George that I was leaving. He begged me to stay and started making the usual hollow promises that he would give up the drink. But I wasn't falling for it this time; I was determined to go back to Los Angeles, to the old life that I knew and loved. Come Monday morning, I was sitting on a flight to Los Angeles once more, leaving George Best and London thousands of miles behind me.

On a yacht in Florida, shortly after our romance had begun.

Above Madly in love in London, 1976.

Left Before the drinking had become too much of a problem, LA, 1977.

Right Fort Lauderdale, Florida, 1977.

Below George sleeps off another of his benders on the sofa at our home in Hermosa Beach, Los Angeles, 1977.

Above Drinking with the in-crowd at Tramp, around 1978.

Below Preparing to go on a TV chat show in Belfast, 1979.

Right With Cher at Venice Beach, Los Angeles, 1980.

Below George and me having dinner in San Jose in the autumn of 1980. I was pregnant at the time.

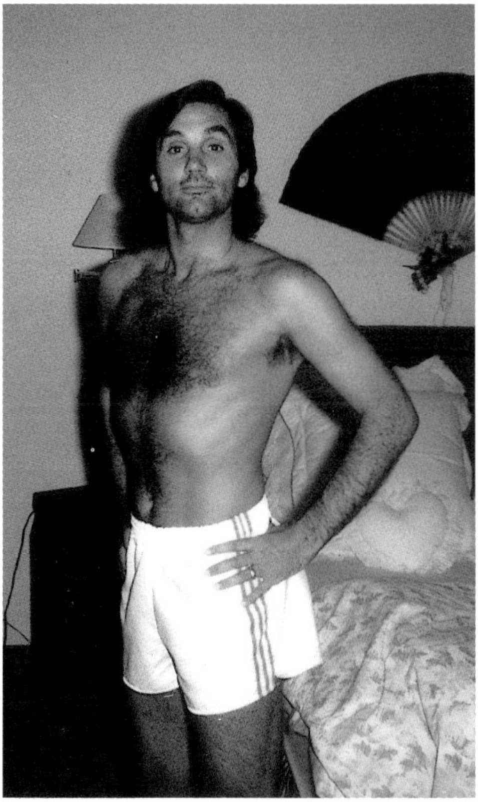

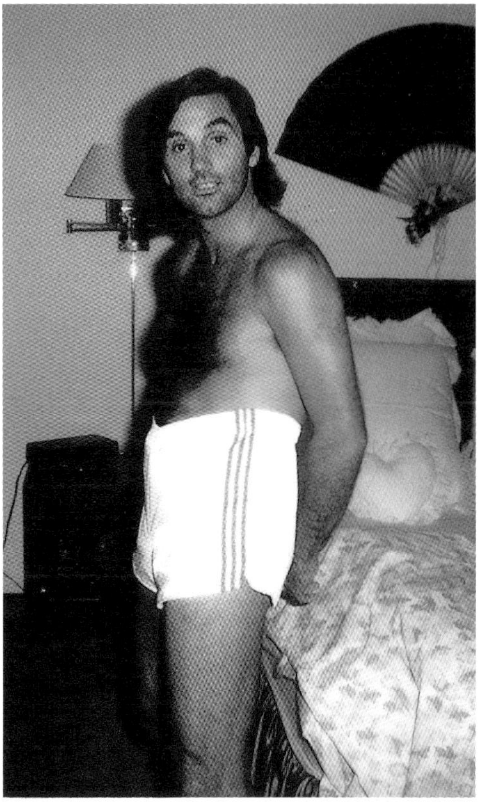

Above George, now aged 34, plays the fool in our bedroom, 1980.

Left George pats my stomach in our jeep in San Jose. Dallas is in the back.
(© *Woman's Own*)

Right Nine months pregnant, San Jose, 1981.

George, sober for once, waiting for the birth
of our son.

8 Playing the Field

'I could tell over the telephone from his slurred speech that George was still drunk, so I didn't say anything because I knew whatever I said would just inflame the situation. He then tried the old trick of telling me how much he loved me and that he wanted to marry me. I just listened and said yes, as by that stage it seemed to be the only way I could get him off the phone.'

CHER, MY SAVIOUR, had pulled me back into her life, which was the life that I loved. Cooped up in my London flat throughout a miserable winter I had been missing the sunshine and the palm trees, and I was so relieved as I boarded that plane. It was as though a huge weight had been lifted from my shoulders: no more dramas, no more drink, no more women. Having said that, by the time the plane touched down in Los Angeles I found His Lordship creeping more and more into my thoughts, but I was determined to resist these feelings and threw myself back into my old life with a vengeance.

I don't think Cher actually believed that I would get on the plane. When I first started seeing George, she hadn't understood what the attraction was. She used to ask me all the time, 'What on earth do you see in him?' We both knew that there were other handsome, famous, rich men interested in me, and Cher always wanted to know why I wouldn't give them a chance. But then, Cher had never met George. When she finally did, at her Beverly Hills home, from that moment on she understood. She simply turned to me and said, '*Now* I see what all the fuss is about.' Even Cher, this huge superstar who was used to people fawning all over her, got caught up in George's web. He just had this presence when he walked into a room, it was electric. He might have been a small man but he would light up a room. Cher picked up on this straight away because she had the same kind of presence. That's why when she rang me in London she assumed George would talk me into staying with him, so when I actually arrived at her house, she was over the moon.

I lost no time contacting all my other old friends, including Josephine, and soon it was as if I had never left. No sooner had my plane touched down than Cher whisked me off to a party at Hugh Hefner's house. We were both a little nervous and very giggly because neither of us had been to one of his infamous parties before and we didn't really know what to expect. We certainly weren't expecting to end up watching a porn movie! Anyway, we socialised a little bit and Cher introduced me to the comedian Bill Cosby, who took an instant liking to me. He invited me to go with him and his friend Muhammad Ali to Lake Tahoe for the weekend where he would teach me how to ice skate. Of course I refused the invitation as I hardly knew the man, but Bill was very insistent, so to avoid his calls I spent the weekend at Josephine's. On the Monday I discovered that he'd sent me some flowers, but, sitting on the doorstep in direct sunlight, they had wilted over the weekend – as did my very brief liaison with Bill Cosby.

My life was once again back on track. I stayed with Cher at her house on Linden Drive in Beverly Hills. We were preparing to go on the road, so it was a very hectic time. We changed the living-room space into a gym so that we could work out every day. Working out was important for Cher not just for fitness and looks, but because the aerobics encouraged her lungs to be efficient, strong enough to enable her to sing while she was dancing. The only real preparation open to performers in those days was exercise; diet had not yet assumed the vital importance it has today. Despite the busy schedule, we always found time to relax, shopping on Rodeo Drive, which was nothing like it is today. In 1977 it was like a little village with a handful of shops where everyone knew everyone else and there was not a camera-snapping tourist to be seen.

I had a fabulous job and was surrounded by people who cared about me, but still I felt that something was not quite right. Then His Lordship called to tell me how much he was missing me. While he was on the phone he started crying, which was not like George at all. Of course, then I started to feel the pangs of guilt for abandoning him. But the guilt soon turned to anger when George went on to accuse me of cheating on him. He said he had a feeling I was fooling around with someone else. I could hardly believe the cheek of the man! There he was, being seen out on the town every night in London with a different woman on his arm – I knew he was still doing this because my family would see him in the newspapers and tell me about it – and he had the nerve to accuse me of seeing another man behind his back! If the truth be told, at that particular stage of my life dating and seeing other men was the last thing on my mind, but of course I didn't give His Lordship the satisfaction of knowing that.

But the anger soon melted. It did not matter if I was in the same room as him or on the other side of the Atlantic, George always had the same effect on me. He began to apologise profusely again and to tell me that he loved me. Then he took me completely by surprise by asking me to marry him. This was the first time George had ever asked me anything remotely like this, although it wouldn't be the last. I refused to believe him, and told him that while I was perhaps prepared to give him one more chance, I would not marry him. Well, George got very angry when I said that and hung up the phone in a fit of madness, then called back ten minutes later to say he was sorry, and we made up over the phone. These little games, which seem so silly to those not emotionally involved, happened constantly while we were apart. George would call me, he would get upset, we would argue, he would hang up, then he would call back and apologise and I would forgive him. In the end it just got ridiculous.

I tried to put our conversation and George's proposal out of my mind when Cher invited me to one of the roller-skating parties she was hosting. Now this was the late 1970s, and roller disco was the latest trend. And when Cher threw a party, everyone turned up. Cher loved fast cars, and at the time she had a gleaming new Ferrari. I remember holding on for dear life as we flew around the winding roads of Malibu Canyon at speeds of up to ninety miles an hour to get to the skating rink. I had no idea what to expect when we got there, and didn't really know who half the people were. But that evening I was introduced to one of the most well-known and hard-partying guys in Hollywood, Jack Nicholson. Well, he took one look at my body, which was super-fit after all the working out I'd been doing with Cher (I weighed just 110 pounds at the time), and the blonde hair and that was that.

Now everyone has heard the stories about Jack – his wild partying, the girls and the drinking – but that night he seemed to me one of the most charming men on the face of the earth. This was around the time that movies such as *One Flew Over the Cuckoo's Nest* and *Chinatown* were creating a real buzz in Hollywood, and Jack could have had his pick of any girl in the room, or any girl in Hollywood for that matter. I'm not so sure that it was my looks as much as the air I gave off that I was not interested in male company that attracted Jack. Even though I had been having rows over the phone with George, I loved him and knew that at some point we would get back together, so I really was intending to remain faithful. I wasn't giving off any vibes of availability, not even to Jack Nicholson. But he was very persistent. He spent all night talking to and flattering me, and by the end of the evening I gave him, when he asked for it, my phone number.

I certainly did not expect to hear from Jack again, but the following evening the phone rang. I picked it up expecting it to be George, but when I heard Jack's distinctive tones down the line it was a big shock. We chatted for a while and he asked me out for dinner the following week, and I found myself saying yes. As I put the phone down I justified it to myself by saying, 'George is five thousand miles away, it's only a dinner.' So I went out for dinner with Jack and had a fabulous time. He was charming, witty company and that sly smile of his had me captivated all evening. The only sad thing he said the whole evening was that in his opinion the best thing he had to offer women was money, which I did not think was true. I'm sure that in his way Jack was just fishing for compliments, but to hear him talking about himself so dismissively still upset me. He had so much more than just money. The next day he sent me a dozen yellow roses. I was delighted with them. George had never sent me flowers in all the time I had known him, yet here was a man who after just one date was sending me a bunch of the most gorgeous roses I had ever seen, and a very sweet note.

I was on such a high – then George called again and all of a sudden my happy, carefree mood evaporated. He told me that he was coming to Los Angeles to play for the Aztecs (he still had a summer-months contract with them, and the 1976/77 English season had just finished) and wanted to see me. I agreed to meet him at the ground, but after the match George was his usual self. I had given up my afternoon to go and watch him play, but the minute the match finished he turned round and told me, 'I don't know why you're here. I'm going to a party tonight with the boys. I'll see you later.' Then he disappeared and left me standing there feeling, and looking, like a complete idiot. There was nothing I could do, so I just went home. Several days later, after he had resurfaced presumably, he rang again. Boy, was he mad. Someone had told him that I was dating Jack Nicholson and the singer Rod Stewart, with whom His Lordship was friends at the time.

Rod was soccer-mad and would sometimes go and play with George in an Aztecs training-session match, and when he saw me again that summer he began to call me. Everyone knows that Rod has a thing for blondes and, well, I was blonde, so I guess he decided I should be next on the list. Again, I felt a bit uncomfortable accepting his dinner invitation, mainly this time because he was a friend of George's, but I did and he took me to a Moroccan restaurant called Dah Magreb where we sat cross-legged and bare-footed to eat. I liked Rod as a person, but it never once crossed my mind that I'd like to start a relationship with him, but that did not stop someone telling His Lordship about our one evening out together.

I could tell over the telephone from his slurred speech that George was still drunk, so I didn't say anything because I knew whatever I said would just inflame the situation. He then tried the old trick of telling me how much he loved me and that he wanted to marry me. I just listened and said yes, as by that stage it seemed to be the only way I could get him off the phone. Within seconds of my putting down the phone, it was ringing again. This time it was Rod, asking me to go and watch him in the recording studio the following day. After that long, badgering call from George I was in the mood to give His Lordship a flea in the ear, so I said yes. I just didn't care whether or not George found out. He was due back in England within a matter of weeks anyway.

I wasn't going to be around for much longer either, because Cher had asked me to go to New York with her for a few months while she was on tour there, and again I jumped at the chance. We had a fabulous time in the Big Apple, working out during the day then living it up at night. On my birthday, 26 July, Cher took me to see a play at the theatre featuring Al Pacino. Afterwards we went backstage and Cher was flirting up a storm with Al. Then, to finish off the evening, we went to the famous nightclub Studio 54, where all the guys hit on us on the dance floor. It was a scream! Jack was also calling me constantly while I was in New York, but I think he'd finally got the message and soon after that lost interest. After all, I was a long way away from him and there were plenty of other young girls nearer to home who doted on him. (But he didn't forget me. When I saw him many, many years later, he laughingly reprimanded me for 'marrying that little soccer player'.)

Then George called with yet another proposal. Again I just dismissed him, for two reasons: I didn't believe he was sincere about wanting to marry me and I didn't trust him – and how can any woman marry a man she doesn't trust? (And I was right to suspect him when he tried that line:

when we did make up and get back together, there would never be any mention of a wedding until I ditched him for a second time and he once again found himself phoning for forgiveness.)

There was another reason for my refusal to consider marriage at that time. My mother had called me in New York to tell me about a little story that had been splashed all over the front of the British newspapers: His Lordship was seeing an old girlfriend, one of his little girls from Hermosa Beach by the name of Heidi. Now, the thing about George was that he was never discreet about these other women of his, and the reason my mother believed these newspaper stories was because they were accompanied by a photograph of the pair of them together. So while he was declaring his undying love for me, once again His Lordship was showing off this other girl around London. To top it off, I got this bizarre transatlantic call from Heidi herself one night asking me for some advice about George. Apparently they had just been out to a club and Heidi had left early, which had proved to be a mistake because George had got more and more drunk and brought another girl home with him. Heidi, close to tears, was now calling me from the living room of the flat while George and this other girl were rolling around in the bedroom. She just didn't know what to do. I told her: 'You can either leave right now or stay and choose to ignore it, because that's just the way George is.'

I don't know for certain which part of my advice Heidi took, but I assume she left him there and then because just two days after that phone call George was on my doorstep in New York insisting that he wanted to spend the rest of his life with me. It was certainly a big step forward from hanging on the other end of the telephone, and a much more romantic gesture, and I was touched by it. We went out for dinner and for the first time we actually sat down and talked properly and level-headedly about our prospects. I was overjoyed that finally, after holding out for it for so long, I was getting a taste of the good side of His Lordship I knew was there. We had a great evening together, deciding that George should go back to London and that I would join him at a later date, either there or in Los Angeles depending on his footballing commitments, after I finished working on the tour with Cher. He promised to behave himself and started making all these grand plans for us, and I was swept up by the excitement of the moment. It's always easy to say with the benefit of hindsight that I should have known George's promises would, in all probability, be shortlived, but when you love someone, although you try to be careful, you do cling on to these moments in your relationship, forever hoping for the best.

Three days after His Lordship arrived in London I called him and he was so drunk he could hardly speak. But, as I'd said to Heidi, that was just the way George was, and I carried on making my plans to join him. I spent the last few weeks of the summer relaxing in the Hamptons on the East Coast with Cher, and in September I flew to Los Angeles, where George was at the time. Of course, I had to get a cab to his place on my own. I had only been there fifteen minutes when Heidi arrived. I answered the door and she just walked in, straight past me. As I stood there thunderstruck, George grabbed her hand and whisked her off into the bedroom for some privacy. I knew they weren't having sex – there are limits to how brazen you can be – because I could hear their voices. George was trying to explain to Heidi why I was there. So I sat down in the living room and twiddled my thumbs, waiting for the two of them to emerge. This dragged on for about twenty minutes. In the end I got so fed up that I grabbed my things and left them to it. (George's Aztecs room-mate Bobby McAlinden later told me that George had said that he thought allowing me to leave that day was the biggest mistake of his life.)

George called me the next day and said 'Hi!' as if nothing had happened. I gave him short shrift. I was still stewing about the Heidi situation and had made up my mind that it was all over again. I had decided to steer clear of men for ever and was determined to have some great girlfriends-only nights out to take me out of myself. And I did, but when you least want to meet someone, anyone, that someone who spins your head pops up at exactly that time in your life. It's always the way, isn't it?

Cher's sister, Georganne, had booked a table at this wonderful restaurant called Mr Chow's and had taken me out to dinner to cheer me up. There we were having a quiet meal, minding our own business, when, on my way to the ladies' room, I bumped into this amazingly gorgeous guy. Just one look at him and it seemed as if all my determination and resolve to stay away from men just melted. He was so good-looking; there was something so refined about him. Ricci Martin was a world away from George in every way possible, and I quickly fell head over heels for him.

9 Livin' La Vida Loca

'George had written me a letter, addressed to Cher's house, telling me how much he missed me, how worried he was about me and how desperately he had been trying to find me. He had cut the letter into the shape of a heart, which of course just melted mine when I saw it because I thought it was such a sweet thing to do.'

RICCI MARTIN WAS a gentleman. Compared with George, he was a saint. He was a Hollywood child, a movie star's son, with class, manners, taste and money. He went everywhere in limousines. There were no dramas, no drinking and definitely no other women lurking in the bedroom. George and Ricci were like night and day. It was such a refreshing change to be with someone who was more interested in me than the bottom of a glass.

When I first bumped into Ricci I had no idea who he was or who his father was – I just thought he was one of the cutest men I had ever seen. I only found out who his famous father was when he took me to his beautiful home on the beach and started playing the piano and singing to me. When he told me his dad was Dean Martin, one of the original members of the Rat Pack and a fabulous singer, I mused, 'Oooh, so that's why he sings so well!' Dean had passed that quality on to his son. Ricci had a wonderful voice. He also had a lovely mother, Jeannie, who extended her hospitality to me one evening when she invited me to a Christmas tree decorating party. It was a lovely evening and a beautiful tree, and I very much liked Ricci's sister Gina too.

After meeting Ricci that night in Mr Chow's, we became almost inseparable. We spent as much time together as we could. We would take long walks along the beach and spend evenings curled up together on the sofa. Ricci loved going to good restaurants, but unlike George he was not into nightclubs or bars. I was taken to Las Vegas to meet his father and hear him sing; I had such a marvellous time that when we went backstage afterwards I felt as though the earth I was standing on was not the same earth Dean was standing on (if you know what I mean!). At the start of the relationship I felt guilty that I was having so much fun. The sense of a huge burden having been lifted was immense. No longer did I have to keep looking over my shoulder every time we went out to see if there was someone around waiting to start a fight; no longer did I have to keep an eye out for women flirting with my partner from the other side of a room. When I was with Ricci, I was the only woman he looked at. It was such a novelty for me. I lapped it up.

During the early days of my relationship with Ricci, it really helped that I did not speak to His Lordship for nearly a fortnight. That might not seem a long time to anyone else, but to me it was for ever. It was the longest time we had had no contact whatsoever, and to be honest, for the first time since I met him George was not even in my thoughts. But that all changed one afternoon when Ricci took me to the Tudor House in Santa Monica, an English tearoom and shop where you can buy all sorts of British food like Kit-Kats and Crunchies and digestive biscuits. That was a big mistake. Being there around British accents acted as a trigger and got me thinking about you-know-who. Ricci, of course, had had no idea of the effect such an environment could have on me because at that stage I hadn't told him about George. All he knew was that I had broken up with someone in London. I began to long to hear His Lordship's voice. Then, almost by coincidence, two days later, he called me at Cher's house.

I had moved back in with Cher because we were working out together every day, but I never for one moment thought that George would call me there. But out of the blue he did, and we had a nice chat. He was like his old, good self, charming and funny. I was firm with him though and told him that I was not coming back to London and that I did not want to see him yet. I didn't mention

Ricci to him as I had only been seeing him for a few weeks, didn't know what was going to happen, and it would only complicate matters anyway.

After I put the phone down, I thought about what I was going to do. The sensible side of my nature urged me to stay with Ricci, with whom there would be no dramas or drunken episodes. Life was peaceful and normal with him, a state of being I had been trying to attain for years. Yet since that afternoon in the tearoom, I just could not stop thinking about His Lordship. To take my mind off everything after the call, I turned on the television. Would you believe it, there was Desi Arnaz Jr. So I was dating Ricci, George was calling me and my old boyfriend Desi was on the box, which just about summed up my feelings of confusion that day! And as if I didn't have enough to think and worry about, I was also at that time trying to be a crutch for Cher, who was going through some problems with Greg. It was almost like looking in a mirror as I watched Cher and Greg argue: they would row, Greg would storm off and then not come home; when he eventually resurfaced he would start on Cher again, like His Lordship used to do with me. Of course, Cher turned out to be stronger than me: when, eventually, she'd had enough, she kicked him out for good.

But in November 1977, Cher and Greg were doing the Allman (Greg's surname) and a Woman tour promoting a great album they did together. I went to Rotterdam in Holland with Cher as part of the tour, and while we were on the road I called Ricci every day. Absence did make my heart grow fonder. I missed him terribly, so I would spend hours on the phone chatting to him. Somehow His Lordship found out that we were on tour, managed to get the number of our hotel and called me there one night. I was surprised but secretly pleased to hear from him. Even though I felt I was starting to fall in love with Ricci, there was still that largely indefinable something pulling me back to His Lordship, despite knowing almost certainly deep down that George would only end up causing me misery while life with Ricci would be near perfect.

Now I know most women who are reading this will probably be screaming at me: why didn't you pick Ricci? And I so wanted to do that, but His Lordship was my first love, and he held sway, for better or worse, over my emotions. Ricci was the safe option, but all women like a little bit of a bad boy, even though in his Lordship's case there was no 'little bit' about it. Other than saying that I truly loved him, the only way I can explain the impulse to move in George's direction is that fate had plans for the two of us, which included having a beautiful child. I know it sounds silly, but it's the only way I can truly rationalise it. I believe to this day that my unborn son was somehow orchestrating our reunion; whatever lessons he had to learn in his lifetime, Calum needed me and George for a mother and father. In that sense, in 1977 our relationship hadn't gone full circle; as soon as it had, and Calum was born, things were finished between us.

But when George called me and said he wanted to meet me in Paris, which was one of our stopping-off points, I was still just about kicking against fate and I told him I would be too busy to see him, but that I would come back to England the day after the Paris leg of the tour ended, in late November. He then began excitedly talking about marriage again, and this time he really sounded serious. I calmed him down and said we would discuss it when I saw him as I was so used to him making wedding plans and nothing happening. Later that day, Ricci called me. He also told me he loved me and missed me and that we should spend the rest of our lives together. Well, now I was in a complete quandary. There were two men in my life, both of whom wanted me, and despite weighing up all the pros and cons of both relationships I still couldn't pick between them. In fact, the only thing I knew for sure is that I would meet up with George in England – or so I thought.

I arrived back in London but, surprise, surprise, there was no sign of His Lordship at the airport, despite the plans we had made. I should have bailed out there and then for good and got straight back on a plane to Ricci. But no, I had to go looking for George. He, of course, had done one of his usual disappearing tricks and was on a bender, which meant the wedding plans went straight out of the window (again). Feeling dejected, I called Ricci who was delighted to hear my voice and spent half an hour telling me how much he wanted to see me. I arranged my ticket back to Los Angeles, but then His Lordship crawled out of a drunken hole somewhere and came to see me. He told me that he was checking into Greyshott Hall, a health farm, to recuperate and sober up. I wearily told him that that was great news, but that it was too late, I was on my way back home to California. And I stuck to my guns.

Ricci was there to meet me at the airport in Los Angeles and he drove me home to Cher's house. I was so pleased to see him. Everything he did that day, everything about him just highlighted for me how inconsiderate and thoughtless George was. So I was pretty well convinced I had finally made my decision – until Ricci asked me to move in with him, and I hesitated. I knew I cared deeply for this man, but something was holding me back from committing to him fully. I told him it was too soon in our relationship to be living together, but the truth was I was just unsure.

At the beginning of December, just to turn everything on its head for the umpteenth time, His Lordship, free of any footballing commitments in Britain, flew into Los Angeles, thus setting off the whole George-or-Ricci debate in my head again. I *knew* His Lordship was bad for me, I *knew* Ricci was the sweetest man I could wish to meet, but whichever way I looked at it I felt I was being drawn with just that bit more power back to His Lordship – and as a consequence of that I lied to Ricci for the first time. I felt awful when I told him that I was going to see a girlfriend, when really I was sneaking off to meet His Lordship, and so I should have done. Ricci believed me, he was so sweet-natured and trusting. If that had been His Lordship, there would have been an interrogation and a shouting match.

But that wasn't an end to the matter. Just before Christmas I came to my senses again – albeit briefly. I was having dinner with His Lordship in a public restaurant where I hoped he would not make a scene, and I told him all about Ricci. For once he sat and listened to me as I poured out the story of my three-month romance, and then I told him that I wanted nothing more to do with him, that Ricci would be better for me in the long run and that I was choosing him. His Lordship confessed then that he had known about Ricci all along: a photo of the two of us had appeared in one of the American tabloids. But he stayed calm and seemed to accept my decision. I breathed a huge sigh of relief. I had expected fireworks across the dinner table but I think because he hadn't been drinking he just seemed to take it all in and for once behaved like an adult.

Of course, this state of affairs didn't last for long. Just days after Christmas, a drunken George was on the phone yelling at me, demanding to know why I hadn't been at home the night before. I had been to a Beach Boys concert with Ricci and had stayed over at his house, but I politely told George that it was none of his business and that I didn't want anything more to do with him. I didn't hear from him for the next few days, so I nervously hoped again that he had accepted my decision.

Early in 1978 I moved out of Cher's house and into my own place. I was still working with her but I wanted somewhere of my own where Ricci could come over and stay and we could be alone together. Everything was going along swimmingly until the middle of January when Cher called me in a panic to let me know that my mother was desperately trying to get hold of me. I called her straight away, thinking that something terrible had happened to her or my sister. As it turned out, she was upset because His Lordship had been constantly bombarding her with phone calls day and night trying to find out where I was.

George had written me a letter, addressed to Cher's house, telling me how much he missed me, how worried he was about me and how desperately he had been trying to find me. He had cut the letter into the shape of a heart, which of course just melted mine when I saw it because I thought it was such a sweet thing to do. I was secretly pleased he had written me such a lovely little letter, but I stiffened my resolve against rashly contacting him. His Lordship, in the absence of a response to his letter, had called Cher who refused to give him my new number. My friend Josephine had also refused to speak to him after I told her not to, so he had resorted to hounding my poor mother in the hope that she would break down and tell him where I had moved to. Initially, my mother also dismissed him and told him that I didn't want to see him at all, but then the calls had got more and more frequent until she couldn't take it any longer. She hadn't wanted to tell me that George had been calling as she didn't want to worry me, but now it had all got too much for her. I rang her and promised her I would call him and sort things out.

I picked up the phone with some trepidation as talking to George was really the last thing I wanted to do. I dialled the number, hoping he wouldn't be in and that I could just leave a message, but he answered after the second ring. The first thing he said was: 'Don't hang up.' I said I wouldn't and he then said he was pleased to hear from me, that he was worried because he hadn't heard from me for three weeks. He sounded like a lost puppy who had just found its owner again, and I felt really pleased with myself for holding back from responding to that letter, which was my way of letting His Lordship know that I was in control. As a consequence, he was now behaving towards me in a calm, considerate way. In fact, he was so impressive in this respect that when he asked if he could come round and see me, I gave him my new address.

His Lordship was there within the hour. As soon as I opened the door he threw his arms around me and gave me the biggest kiss in the world. It seemed like a whole new George standing on my doorstep, one I had never met before but one I definitely wanted to know. All of a sudden, Ricci was out of my mind and His Lordship once more took pride of place. He proposed again, and this time his timing was impeccable. He suggested we fly to Las Vegas immediately. He looked so serious, so proud to be asking me to be his wife, that I said yes on the spot, even though to this day I don't really know what made me agree or why I thought this time things would be any different. His Lordship stayed over, and that night we lay awake making all sorts of plans: buying a house together, raising a family and living happily ever after. I knew what His Lordship was like and how he could never keep his promises, but somehow that night it all felt just right.

The hardest thing about accepting George's marriage proposal was breaking the news to Ricci. I loved Ricci, but nothing could compare to the way I felt when I was with George. I just didn't know how to tell him that George was now my choice – I had a hard enough time rationalising it to myself – but I think he saw it in my face. Leaving Ricci made me realise what a special person he was. I spent most of that day with him, and we both cried as we said our goodbyes.

So here I was ready to start a new, married, life with His Lordship. It is every woman's dream to have the fairytale wedding and live happily ever after, but George is not a traditional or conventional guy and our wedding in a chapel in Las Vegas was a sure sign of things to come.

10 I Do (I Think)

'His Lordship went into the bedroom. I followed him, hoping for a spot of passion to at least liven up the day, but as I walked through the door I did a double-take. Sure, George was taking his clothes off, but he wasn't climbing between the sheets, he was getting changed! I asked him what he was doing and he told me he'd arranged to meet the boys down the pub. I was dumbfounded. It was our wedding night! As he walked out of the door, he said, "Don't wait up".'

When we announced our engagement, my mother Mimi said, 'George Best is hardly any mother-in-law's dream!' Of course, she was right. She was very much in two minds about me marrying His Lordship, and who could blame her? The last contact she'd had with George, he'd been haranguing her for my address and phone number. I remember that when I first told her that I was dating him, she had said to me, 'For goodness' sake Angela, leave that man alone!' She had read all the newspaper articles about George and her view on my news that day was that it was 'not terribly encouraging'. But when she first met him she was bowled over, as so many people were, by his Irish charm.

The first time I took George home to meet my parents, reporters and photographers had been camped outside their home in Southend for two days. For some reason we had been delayed getting there by a day, so my poor parents had had to put up with all these pressmen waiting around outside. As His Lordship and I arrived at the house, chaos erupted. Flashes started going off and everyone began to fire questions at us. My parents quickly ushered us into the house, and amid all the excitement my mother forgot George's name. As His Lordship stood in the kitchen, my mother turned to him and said, 'Do you want a cup of tea? By the way, what's your name, son?' We all thought that was hilarious. The world's most famous footballer was standing in her kitchen and my mother couldn't even remember his name.

George was the perfect guest. He loved to spend weekends at my parents' house, having lunch and then watching the football results with my dad, Joseph. My mother had to reluctantly admit that when he was sober George was 'the nicest man in the world'. Yet she knew that he had two sides to his character. My poor mother only knew half of what I had gone through with George, and still she could see that he was the wrong man to marry.

The wedding itself, on 24 January 1978, was a complete fiasco. I defy anyone to come forward and tell me they had a worse wedding day than mine. I remember running around in a tizzy just trying to find something to wear. In the end I went out and bought an outfit that made me look like a schoolmarm. I found a lovely white jacket, a smart shirt and a nice skirt, but put them all together and I looked like I should be standing in front of a primary school class with some chalk and a ruler in my hand. In fact, the only items of clothing on me that looked vaguely hip and trendy were the shoes, and people rarely notice them in any of the wedding photos because the first thing they are drawn to is my awful hairdo. At the hairdresser's on the morning of the wedding the stylist had decided I should look different for my 'special day', so she curled my hair in rollers. Unfortunately, the result was what could only be described as a frizzed perm. I looked atrocious. And when I showed up at the airport, everybody else thought so too! In fact, His Lordship didn't recognise me at first and walked straight past me. In my defence, he looked no better. As I got closer to George, I realised he hadn't even bothered to wash his hair, which was greasy and clinging to his head, so we both looked terrible, not at all like a happy couple in love.

And that was just prior to the wedding. The whole day was awful, even though when I look back on it I was in a complete daze. I'd never been married before and I'd had absolutely no time to plan anything. I didn't even know you could get people to help you out with things like a dress or a reception. As usual, I was totally clueless. George was the one who wanted to get married so quickly. 'Let's go to Las Vegas and do it now!' he'd said. Everything happened in a blur; I hardly had time to catch my breath. I think His Lordship feared that if we waited any longer I would change my mind again and go back to Ricci (although, knowing George as I do, and taking into account later events, I wouldn't be surprised if the speed of the wedding was down to him being penniless and the thought of all the money he would get via his manager for a Best marriage scoop in the press).

I asked Josephine to be my bridesmaid, so she and her husband John picked me up and off we went to Los Angeles airport. When I got there, I expected George to come over and hug me or kiss me, or at least hold my hand. But he wouldn't come anywhere near me. I was hurt that my husband-to-be appeared to want nothing to do with me and I was about to demand that Josephine take me back home when George's then-manager Ken Adams came over to explain everything. He told me that I couldn't be seen with George, I couldn't stand next to him, I couldn't sit next to him on the plane, I couldn't even say hello.

You see, Ken had sold the story to one of the newspapers as an exclusive (I didn't know you could do something like that in those days!). He had arranged this exclusive deal with the paper and then told George about it, but no one had bothered to tell me until I arrived at the airport. I didn't even know which newspaper was going to print the exclusive, but it was obvious that somehow the cat had got out of the bag because there were pressmen crawling all over the place trying to spoil the scoop by getting pictures of the two of us together. On the plane I had to sit ten rows behind His Lordship when all I really wanted to do was sit next to him and feel his arm around me. When we arrived in Las Vegas we had to take separate cars to the chapel, and we didn't even go straight there. Instead, we hurtled around the town for about two hours trying to lose all the reporters and photographers. It was like a scene out of a Keystone Cops film.

His Lordship later admitted that he had arrived in Las Vegas a little drunk. I hadn't noticed because I was just too wound up worrying about everything else. To be honest, I don't blame His Lordship for wanting a drink to calm his nerves on that particular day. I felt exactly the same, especially when we finally arrived at the Candlelight Wedding Chapel only to find that we didn't have a legal licence to allow us to tie the knot. We didn't know that we needed one, so there we all were, running around like headless chickens trying to get this licence. We finally managed to get one and went back to the chapel. We were a frazzled little entourage. To make matters worse, the priest was a really camp gay guy in an atrocious lime green suit which set me off into hysterical giggles. I just couldn't stop, and His Lordship fired angry glances at me. He often did things like that, trying to burst my bubble.

It wasn't just the priest's clothes; by this stage I was cracking up because the whole day had just been a total and utter fiasco. I was trying desperately to keep a straight face throughout the brief ceremony but all I could focus on was the hilarity of it all. The suit, the cheesy chapel, me and His Lordship literally hating the sight of each other. He was wearing this horrendous American check jacket that looked like someone had done an Irish jig on it – it was dreadful! I think both of us looked the worst we had ever looked in our lives, and to top it all off His Lordship had no wedding rings. He had to borrow one from Bobby McAlinden (his best man) which didn't fit my finger properly (after we got back to Los Angeles I had to take George's gold watch and melt it down to have two matching rings made). So I was giggling through this whole fiasco and the newspaper was taking pictures of us looking like a couple of fashion throwbacks who can't stand the sight of each other. To quote His Lordship, 'The only fortunate thing was that it was all over in about three minutes.' At least we both felt the same way about it.

The so-called reception was just as laughable. The whole thing was so surreal! For all the attention I was able to pay to what was going on, a resurrected Elvis could have been there singing along to the Wedding March. Ken was trying so hard to stage-manage everything to keep the newspaper happy. It took all my efforts just to try to follow his directions – 'Stand here, do this, look that way' – and I hardly had time to take it all in. It all took place in a cheap, tacky, nasty hotel that put on a dreadful buffet, the kind of place where you pay a set fee to eat and drink as much as you like. I remember thinking as we drove from the chapel to the hotel, 'No, this is not right. It all feels so wrong.' The food was practically inedible and no one was really in the right sort of mood to celebrate. It was not like a normal wedding where everyone is toasting the happy couple and there is dancing and cutting of the cake; at our reception, everyone just sat around the table looking subdued. I didn't know what to say to George, and I think he felt pretty uncomfortable too. I certainly didn't feel as if I'd just become someone's wife. In fact, sitting there at the table eating terrible food in a frumpy outfit and a ridiculous hairdo, the only thing I felt was downright embarrassment, that and sadness that my parents weren't there. The wedding arrangements had happened so quickly that we hadn't had time to organise their trip out to America. Then again, thinking back on it, I'm glad they weren't there. I think the experience would have been a big disappointment to my mother especially, to see me wed in that way.

At some point, just when I was beginning to think nothing else could go wrong, a waitress tripped and spilt a whole glass of Coca-Cola all over my white jacket, which pretty much took the biscuit. Little did I know that the *pièce de resistance* was still to come. If I was expecting to spend my first night as a married woman being swept off my feet by my new husband in some fabulous honeymoon suite in one of the hotels along the Las Vegas strip, I was sadly mistaken. Instead, when the pitiful dinner was over, he leant across and whispered in my ear, not the sweet nothings I was hoping and longing to hear, rather a typical George sentence: 'Hurry up, we've got to catch the plane back to Los Angeles in an hour.' So before I knew what had hit me, I was back on a plane. At least this time I was allowed to sit next to His Lordship.

I can laugh at the disastrous nature of the day, but I can get angry too. In some respects George and I were just pawns in the affair, with me the biggest pawn of all. Everybody got what they wanted: the papers had their pictures, Ken got his money, George finally got me to marry him, but what did I get? We arrived home at our little flat and all I could think was: 'Is that it? What happens now?' Well, His Lordship made the decision as to what should happen next: he went into the bedroom. I followed him, hoping for a spot of passion to at least liven up the day, but as I walked through the door I did a double-take. Sure, George was taking his clothes off, but he wasn't climbing between the sheets, he was getting changed! I asked him what he was doing and he told me he'd arranged to meet the boys down the pub. I was dumbfounded. It was our wedding night! As he walked out of the door, he said, 'Don't wait up.'

Imagine the scene. I was standing in the middle of the living room in a cobbled-together white outfit with a big brown Coke stain on the front just hours after marrying the man I loved. My mouth was wide open from shock and he was just about to shut the front door behind him. Eventually my mouth closed, and with that came a familiar deflated feeling. There you go, you've let yourself trust George Best again. There wasn't a hint of a candlelit dinner, not a word of a promise of eternal love, absolutely nothing to mark what should have been the most special night of my life. But then I shouldn't really have expected anything more from His Lordship. He'd always been a simple man with simple tastes.

It was so sad because there I was already regretting getting married. But almost immediately I found myself feeling determined to make it work, even if it was to be an uphill struggle all the way. Maybe it was the Scottish genes in me, but I was going to put my heart and soul into making my marriage a successful one. I naively thought that with enough effort and dedication I could make His

Lordship into the perfect husband. I suppose we all start our married lives with high hopes, ignoring the fact that deep down we know that you can't make somebody into something they don't want to be. Early in 1978 I was 25 years old and idealistic; I wouldn't entertain the thought that George and I would never be a normal couple in any sense of the word. As it turned out, our relationship continued to go up and down more times than a whore's drawers, as they say! One of the main reasons for that was that we rarely did things as a couple. George never arranged anything. The only times we did go out were to parties, dinners or functions somebody else had organised. In London, for instance, we used to get invitations to film premières. One of them, I remember (because I had such a good time), was a movie about footballers called *Yesterday's Heroes*, which all the critics insisted was based on George's life. I thought that was a load of nonsense, but it wasn't a bad film.

The other big reason, of course, was the drink. There wasn't a specific point when His Lordship's drinking became a problem in the marriage, mainly because it had already been a problem for a long time. But it was always a problem I thought I could handle. I couldn't, however, overcome his stubborn Irishness and his self-absorption. His Lordship says that when he goes on a binge he withdraws into solitude: 'It's always been that way, and when I'm on my own I think too much, it makes it worse. I don't talk to anyone, I don't stay, I just skip from place to place until I come to my senses.' Lonely. He was always lonely, but he brought his loneliness on himself because he didn't know how to relate to people.

Before long he wasn't the only one who was lonely in our marriage.

11 The Honeymoon is Over

'In that instant I was witnessing the aftermath of what George would refer to later as a "Coyote Morning". Coyotes, you see, when caught in a trap, will chew their own leg off rather than remain in the jaws of the trap; "Coyote Morning" refers to the fact that a man would rather chew a limb off than wake up the girl he'd slept with as he left because she was so damn ugly.'

I SPENT THE FIRST 24 hours of my married life more in a state of shock than bliss. His Lordship was soon in the usual place at his bar and I was left on my own to begin putting together our new life. I didn't go down to the bar very much myself because it wasn't really my scene, which was a shame because my husband was there every single night. Oh well! I still tried to be the wife that he would want to come home to. I have already explained how I learnt to cook wonderful meals, which usually ended up being fed to our dog, Dallas, who was always a comfort to and a companion for me.

Despite being so loving and convincing when he asked me to marry him, George never really made an effort to make the marriage work. The moment the ring was on my finger, it was as if he gave up any notion of having to be romantic or caring. There were still occasional moments during those first few months when he wouldn't drink for a week here or a week there, and those times were just idyllic. We would spend time together shopping or just hanging out at the beach. I don't think George went out of his way not to drink at those times, it was just that he still went through brief periods when he didn't fancy one. But all too soon he would be back in the bar with the boys.

We spent a good few months in the summer of 1978 in Fort Lauderdale, Florida, while George played for the Fort Lauderdale Strikers; that was another period during which His Lordship pretty much behaved himself. He would go for a drink after a game, but would usually come home at a respectable hour and after only a few of his favourite tipple, vodka. On the few occasions when His Lordship stayed out, I invited Lindy over to stay and she and I behaved like two teenagers ourselves. We would go to Studio 51, the local nightclub, and dance up a sweat with all the local, gorgeous, rich Argentinian boys. This certainly took my mind off His Lordship and all his boring problems! But it was all harmless fun. I remember my sister and I would drive around in my jeep with the roof off, Dallas in the back and the radio blaring out the Hall & Oates song 'Atlanta June', which was my favourite at the time. We would be singing along at the tops of our voices without a care in the world – until we got home, of course.

As soon as we returned to Los Angeles later in the year, the demon drink raised its ugly head again and George started staying out later and later. His Lordship was like a caricature of a nursery rhyme: 'When he was good he was very very good, but when he was bad he was evil.' There was no middle ground with George, it was usually all or nothing – which is how he approached his football as well.

I spent most of that first year of my married life working with Cher and getting the Bests' new beach house into some sort of order. I was able to shut my mind to George's ever-increasing disappearances with an ever-increasing workload. I worked really hard to put together a wonderful little house for him eventually to come home to, for him to *want* to come home to, and everything did indeed sail along on a pretty even keel for a while. I didn't mind the odd binge here and there as it usually put George in a good mood for days afterwards as he tried to suppress feelings of guilt for wandering off again. But as the year drew to a close, one incident threatened to tip me over the edge, and landed George in hospital too.

It was Christmas 1978, and His Lordship had been missing for two days. I wasn't worried at this stage because he had been gone for three or four days in a row before, so I just carried on as usual. But come the end of the first week, I was getting more and more concerned. Christmas came and went. I couldn't believe George had failed to turn up; I was so upset that he had left me on my own during the holidays, and no one seemed to know where to find him. I found it odd and worrying that all the boys in the bar, when I questioned them, denied any knowledge of George's whereabouts because they always knew his movements (even though I knew they all disliked me, regarding me as the woman who was trying to take all the fun out of George when all I really wanted to do was not stop him drinking, but stop him drinking *so much*).

Before long the New Year had come and gone, and by this time my anxiety had turned to anger. I considered going to the police to file a missing persons report. I just had no idea what had happened to His Lordship, and now I was fearful he was lying dead or injured in a ditch somewhere. The problem with George was that when he got completely wasted, he often blacked out and forgot where he was or what he was doing. All that mattered at times like these was finding the next drink, and he could end up literally anywhere. I hadn't seen him now for two weeks, but knowing what he could be like I was getting more and more furious that he had done this to me, rather than worried.

I later found out that he had been with this short, skanky (as my son would say), long-haired waitress from his bar, Bestie's. I didn't know her name, I had never even spoken to her. I had no idea who she was or where she lived, but apparently His Lordship in his state had decided to set up home with her rather than come home to his wife. Perhaps she was keeping him in drink, because we never kept any in the house. That is one thing George never did: drink at home on his own. It wasn't that he was ashamed of his drinking, far from it (although sometimes he should have been!). He never hid his drinking, he was very open about it, but if he wanted a drink he would always go down to the pub and have a vodka or a glass of champagne.

I was fed up with him and wanted to leave. I was in the bedroom getting ready to pack up all my things when I saw Dallas's ears prick up. Just seconds after the dog heard George, I heard His Lordship coming down the path towards the front door. I couldn't really fail to actually, because he was making a hell of a noise. I could tell he was drunk and I was terrified of the mood he might be in. Whenever he came home like that he would always be aggressive and nasty because he would always be angry with himself for being in such a state. His best defence was usually offence at my expense.

On the spur of the moment, I hid myself in the wardrobe in the bedroom, hoping he wouldn't realise I was in and would pass out (and sober up). In a prior drunken incident he had broken the telephone in the living room, so he came into the bedroom to use the phone. He obviously thought he was at home alone because he slumped down on the bed with his back to the wardrobe and began to dial. I don't know to this day what number it was because they didn't have caller ID in those days, but I heard him say in a very slurred voice, 'She's not here. Come and get me. I miss you.'

Well, I didn't just see red, I saw every colour you could possibly imagine. When I heard those words, such a betrayal of everything we had gone through over the last year, I wanted to kill the bastard, but I knew that if I jumped out at him he would probably get the better of me. So I didn't emerge from my hiding-place to begin with, I stayed inside seething and under my breath calling him every name under the sun. I probably could have screamed out those names and he wouldn't have known who said it or where it was coming from, he was so legless. But I wasn't taking any chances.

After he put the phone down, His Lordship got up off the bed and left the room, This was my cue; I could contain myself no longer. As he moved away, I came out of the wardrobe and followed him. Don't ask me why at that point I suddenly thought it would be a good idea to confront him, or why I said the words I said. I just did. I ran after him, shouting, 'George, George, please don't go! Stay here with me!' I shouldn't have resorted to begging him to stay; for one, he was completely plastered, and secondly, I was demeaning myself by doing it, especially since deep down all I wanted was for him to get out of my sight anyway. Such conflicting emotions!

When he realised I was there and had been hiding from him, he got really mad. I was standing in the kitchen listening to this drunken little man yelling at me for being in the house and not telling him, and I thought, 'What on earth are you doing, yelling at me like that? What are you yelling at me for, you prat? *You're* the one who has been gone for a fortnight, *you're* the one who left me alone during Christmas and New Year! No one knew where you were, I was here on my own, and *you* are yelling at *me*?' My mouth was wide open as I stood there in complete disbelief at his attitude. The argument ended with George turning and beginning to stumble off, saying, 'I'm leaving!' I yelled back, 'Fine, leave then!'

But as he walked away, I snapped. We had a block of wood in the kitchen with several carving knives stuck in it. Without thinking, I grabbed one of them, ran into the living room and stuck it right in his bum. I had never in my life done anything remotely like it. I had never so much as harmed a hair on anyone's head before. I hadn't even known that I was capable of doing something like that, and the moment I plunged that knife into my husband's backside, I was totally shocked by my behaviour. All I can say is it was a measure of how completely infuriating George's attitude could be when the demon drink was controlling him. It was the same snap judgement, however poor, I'd experienced outside Tramp the night I smashed up his Jaguar. Just *what* can I do to make an impression on him and get the man to listen to me?

Now it was George's turn to look gobstruck. He grabbed his bum, mumbled some profanities, then looked down at his hands and saw that they were covered in blood. I ran back into the kitchen and flung the bloody knife into the sink. The last thing I wanted was for His Lordship in his state to get his hands on it. When I turned round, I saw that George had picked up an onyx ashtray – a present from a football charity event – which was now also covered in blood. We stood there for a moment, staring at each other, both of us in deep shock, me with my mouth open again, completely mortified, thinking, 'What the hell have I done?' I knew I had stepped way over the line. Blood was dripping off this ashtray on to the floor, and His Lordship was just standing there with it in his hand. He looked from the ashtray to me, and back to the ashtray. Then he swung his arm back and threw it at me with all the strength he had. Luckily, it was a drunkard's throw and I managed to duck out of the way. It hit a cupboard door and broke it. All I can remember thinking in the moments after that was, 'Oh my God, there's blood everywhere! How am I going to get it out of the carpet?' I had never seen so much blood before. Thankfully, with that throw it seemed His Lordship had spent himself, and he staggered out of the front door, leaving a little trail of blood behind him.

I quickly regained my composure and began to clean up the blood. It never once crossed my mind to follow him out on to the street to see if he was all right; once he left, my anger returned and I was far more preoccupied with picking up where I had left off. So I continued packing up all my things and called the removal men. And I needn't have worried about His Lordship. George later told me that after he left the house he had walked down to the end of the street where the waitress had picked him up. They both went to a nearby hospital where he had the wound in his bum stitched up. He said he'd told the nurse that he'd sat down on a piece of glass without realising it was there. She'd probably taken one look at him and thought, 'Well, you're drunk enough. I suppose anything could have happened.'

I still don't know to this day who that waitress was. But it's not about who she was or who any of them were. They were just warm bodies as far as George was concerned, warm bodies that gave him the attention he craved. He just had a need. It didn't matter about anybody or anything, he just had to feed this need to have a warm body next to him when he was drunk. This may sound odd, but it really wasn't a personal thing, and I didn't see it like that. The reason I got angry with him wasn't the usual reason – because he was being unfaithful – rather that he always seemed to be trying to do his level best to screw things up for us. It wasn't as if he was out looking for what he wasn't getting at home after all, he just wanted someone near him to stop him feeling lonely when he was drunk and he always picked the nearest woman (he never drank at home, remember). It didn't even matter what she looked like, as I found out later on several occasions when I disturbed him.

On the morning of one of those occasions I was looking for His Lordship and walked into our apartment, which at that time he was sharing with a few of the boys because I had temporarily moved out. I walked into our bedroom and found Ken Adam, George's manager, there, and he told me that George was in another room. I tried the next bedroom with a double bed, thinking that would be the most likely place to find him, but there was a snoring footballer between the sheets. I just couldn't imagine for one minute that His Lordship would be in the bedroom with the single bed in it. Silly me! Lo and behold, as I opened the door, there was George, stark naked, about to climb into the single bed. In that instant I was witnessing the aftermath of what he would refer to later as a 'Coyote Morning'. Coyotes, you see, when caught in a trap, will chew their own leg off rather than remain in the jaws of the trap; 'Coyote Morning' refers to the fact that a man would rather chew a limb off than wake up the girl he'd slept with as he left because she was so damn ugly.

Anyway, the waitress took His Lordship to the hospital and the removal men came to the apartment, took all my stuff away and put it in storage. I left a note for George telling him that I had gone. I took all my plants to Ricci's house because I knew he would look after them and I knew I could still count on him when anything went wrong. He tried to talk me into staying with him, but I knew I needed to be on my own for a while so I went over to Cher's and she told me I could stay as long as I liked.

Ricci began calling me there every day, which was really good for my self-esteem. I decided, probably wrongly, to spend a few days with him. He understood that I only wanted to be friends while I sorted myself out, but he assured me he would always be there to console me, talk to me, take care of me, let me be self-indulgent and not expect anything back. He was such a sweet man. Ricci always listened and never turned me away.

I was at Ricci's one day a week or so later when the phone rang. It was George. It was then I realised that the phone bill must have arrived. He had obviously finally gone home to the one bed and one chair I had left him (that's all I figured he'd need, the amount of time he actually spent there) and seen the bill. Usually I had been very discreet whenever I felt the need to talk through my problems with Ricci. I would walk down the road to a pay phone so the number wouldn't show up on the bill and cause George any unnecessary grief. But the day of the stabbing, in my shock, I had called Ricci from the house. His Lordship now had his number.

As usual after a bender, with guilt weighing him down, George was all husband-like on the phone. 'You're married to me,' he said. 'I'm coming to get you, you're coming home.' I explained to him that I was staying at Cher's, not Ricci's, that I was just over there to thank Ricci for being such a good and understanding friend – which is what he was. That didn't make any difference to George. Once he got an idea into his head, there was no stopping him. Impatience started to take hold, and he told me to get my things together at Cher's, but I told him I wasn't coming home. I then called Cher and warned her that he might turn up on the doorstep. He did.

For the next few days I was walking around on eggshells, expecting George to burst through the front door at Ricci's place at any moment; Cher was in a similar situation at her house. Cher had moved to the Malibu Colony, a group of mansions mainly owned by celebrities set in a gated community with guards patrolling the grounds 24 hours a day. Then, as I was driving home from Ricci's, rounding a corner near the Colony I saw someone sitting on the kerb. I suddenly realised that the dishevelled-looking creature on the side of the road was none other than His Lordship. The minute he saw me, he stood up and ran towards the jeep. I was terrified; I still didn't want anything to do with him. So I sped off, His Lordship running after me. He seemed to be angry with me, so I didn't even slow down. Then I caught a glimpse of him in my rear-view mirror and immediately started to feel tremendously sorry for him. He looked so drawn and pathetic. I turned the jeep round and went back. When I got to him I said straight away, 'Please, George, don't do anything.' But I don't think anything of the sort was on his mind. He was obviously coming down from a bender, not in the middle of one, and all of a sudden he started crying, telling me between the sobs how sorry he was for everything he had done to me.

Once again, the mother in me took over and I drove him back to our house in Hermosa Beach. By the time we arrived he had started to get the shakes. I tucked him into bed and he started having really bad withdrawals. I later found out that he had been on a bender for nearly two weeks and was in a really bad way. After I had hung up the phone on him at Ricci's, George had decided he needed to find me, had broken into the Malibu Colony (so much for the 24-hour guards!) and had sneaked around trying to find Cher's house. He had spent the whole day crawling through bushes and climbing over fences trying to find the right house, and during that time he had not had a single drink. I was gobsmacked when he told me this. He was lucky not to have got himself shot. This was a celebrity enclave – Barbra Streisand lived across the street from Cher, Neil Diamond up the road – and the private security guards would not have hesitated to shoot if they thought the threat warranted it. At the very least they would have thrown him into prison if they'd caught him. The silly little bugger.

I stayed by his side as he fought to get over the shakes. I fed him soup and tried to get him straight again. Not once during this time did any of the boys he hung around with call in to see how he was. They didn't really care about George, or about what happened to him. They wanted to be his friend and drinking buddy, that's all. They would rather get another round in and carry on chatting than say to him, 'George, you're going to kill yourself, you've got to stop drinking like that.' Instead they just let him get on with it, buying him drink after drink, leaving me to mop up the mess every time. And I always did.

The attitude of his male 'friends' in Britain was just as bad, if not worse (if that's possible). I remember one night later on in 1979 George was at one of his pubs with some acquaintances drinking champagne and I was supposed to go there, pick him up and drive us both to the health farm Greyshott Hall for a much-needed rest on my part and for drying out on his. I arrived at the pub and of course George and his mates were in the middle of a session. I waited patiently, but I knew Greyshott Hall closed its doors at midnight so by eleven o'clock I was in a complete panic to leave. I pleaded with the men, 'Please, let me take George,' and I explained that we were going to a health farm as he needed to dry out (or at least moderate his drinking – the best you could hope for, really) for a bit. 'Yeah, yeah, Ange,' one of them said. I boldly started walking George towards the door when another one grabbed his arm and said, 'Come on George, just one more bottle.' They couldn't have cared less about George's welfare, just the gratification of their own egos.

His Lordship and I used to go to Greyshott Hall all the time. It was more of a mental help for George (and an effective one) as it usually put him in the right frame of mind so far as drinking was concerned. While we were there we would sometimes sneak off to a pub called the Links to eat prawns and drink champagne – along with everyone else who was supposed to be at Greyshott, of course – but this was sociable drinking, not excessive, lonely drinking; there was a world of difference between the two and it did His Lordship good. We both have fond memories of Greyshott Hall, and it became the scene for some wonderful stories, especially the one when George went off for a jog and ran into the nearest town to buy me some chocolates. By the time he got back to the spa he was out of breath, so he put the chocolates down to get himself a glass of water, but when he turned around the chocolates had been nicked!

It took George several days to get over the shakes. He'd been as sick as a dog, mainly because he hadn't eaten anything for two weeks. It was pathetic really; he was just like a little baby. But I was his wife now, I knew his so-called 'friends' abandoned him at times like this, so I thought it my duty to care for him. And I did.

12 What a Plank!

'Once again the familiar routine began to kick in. George started to miss training at Hibernian, and of course it wasn't long before they were forced into showing him the door. It was such a shame because everyone always showed willing to keep on giving George a chance, but there were limits and His Lordship always managed to reach them.'

STABBING HIS LORDSHIP was the only time I ever made the first violent move during an argument after George had been drinking. At the time I was horrified with myself that I could have physically harmed anyone. I know he had severely provoked me, but what I did was still way out of order. Although I left the house after the incident, it was never in my mind that it would be permanent. His Lordship was only like that when he was drunk, and if he ever hit me it was because of that; he never once raised his hand to me when he was sober, and I was still determined to make our marriage work.

There was another time – the only other time – when I fought back, but that was strictly in self-defence, in an attempt to stop His Lordship from going too far. It was early September 1979, and we were staying in a hotel on the beach, just down from Bestie's. We had packed up all our stuff as George had been offered a job with Hibernian Football Club; we were moving back to the UK and had a few days to spare before our flight. I went down to the beach with George for breakfast and we had a nice chat and began making plans about what we would do when we got to Scotland. Suddenly George got up from the table and told me he would be back in a few minutes. I assumed he had gone to the bathroom, but two hours later there was still no sign of him. I searched the hotel without any luck. I began to get nervous. I was pretty sure His Lordship had gone off to top himself up, and I knew that with a plane to catch later in the day, trouble was probably brewing.

I sat and looked out of the hotel window which faced down on to the beach, an old habit. I always used to sit and look out of a window and wait for his car to come home no matter where we lived. Then I saw His Lordship walk along the beach and pop his head into the café. Obviously I was no longer there, but instead of coming up to the room, he turned around and headed off down the road. I ran downstairs to see if I could catch up with him but when I got outside he was long gone. I knew there was no point in going down to the bar at that stage because when His Lordship wanted to have a drink, he had a drink and there was no stopping him. Well, two hours of walking along the beach later I went back up to our room, but still no George. I called the bar about an hour after that and Bobby McAlinden confirmed he was in there. George came on the phone but was very defensive and told me he was going to stay there for a few more drinks. I warned him that we had a plane to catch and pleaded with him not to be late, but I didn't push too hard because he sounded as drunk as a skunk. I sat down on the bed and carried on watching the television. My stomach was so twisted up I couldn't face going outside and speaking to people.

The next thing I knew, His Lordship came barging into the hotel room, wanting to pick a fight. We were yelling and screaming at each other, as usual when he was paralytic, but then George came at me. In the ensuing struggle my lip and my neck were hurt. I hadn't done a thing other than shout back at him, but then when His Lordship was in the mood I didn't have to do anything to provoke his aggression. He would just be angry at himself for being in such a state and be looking to blame the nearest person. At one point he turned his back on me, so I picked up a two-inch wide plank of wood – which was just sitting in the hotel room for some ungodly reason – and hit him over the head with it, hoping to knock him out. I really whacked him with it, but to little effect. Instead he just turned around and pushed me away. I sat on the floor where I landed and cried. George lay down on the couch. Several hours later he started to sober up and was very apologetic. He was like a different person, and later I was to learn that alcoholics always are. He even went out to the supermarket and got us something to eat because I couldn't go anywhere with a swollen lip. In fact, I looked like death warmed up. Needless to say, we didn't manage to get on the flight that night, so we rearranged to fly the following day. I spent all the intervening time scared as I feared he might just disappear, repeat the scene and miss the plane again, but George remained as good as gold. He had a few vodkas in the airport bar, but we made the flight without a problem.

Relating this incident now makes me realise how innocent (or stupid) I really was all those years ago. Whenever George stayed off the drink and behaved himself, I made such a fuss of him for being good that all the bad things he had done just hours or days before went straight out the window. I always seemed to put the horrific moments to one side, like I did in January 1983 when we were both in London but had separated. I was in Tramp enjoying a night out with some girlfriends. George was in there too, completely drunk and in a very bad mood, so before he could cause a scene I left and went home. A few hours later he came over to my house. I usually put the chain on, but hadn't on this night, although I knew that if I didn't let him in he would just knock the door down anyway. I knew it would be easier to let him in, give him a cup of tea and then let him go on his merry way, but on this occasion he would not leave.

He got into my bed but, fearful that he would vomit or pass out and I would be stuck with him all night, I told him he had to leave. At this, His Lordship rolled off the bed, grabbed me roughly by the neck and pulled my hair. The minute he let go I called the police. Then I called his girlfriend at the time, the former Miss World Mary Stavin, to tell her what he had done, but I only managed to get into an argument with her too! By the time the police arrived George had slunk off, so I just told them to forget it. I said it was just a stupid domestic argument, and they left. You see, I just couldn't bring myself to have him arrested. And sure enough, the minute he sobered up he was on the phone to apologise.

When I first met George the drinking hadn't been that much of a problem, but through 1978 and 1979 it was getting worse and worse. Being left alone on my own for days at a time didn't bother me as it might have bothered some women, but I was increasingly becoming fearful of and for George, the man I was in love with who was slowly disappearing into a bottle. And I repeat: not once did I think about leaving him for good, and looking back on my experiences now I can honestly say I don't know why. Normal women would probably have run a mile from a man like that, but it never entered into my thoughts. And it was not as if I was a little plain Jane sitting in the corner with no one else interested in me. The thing was, when I exchanged vows with George and I said 'for better or for worse', I truly meant it, and I was not going to give in. In addition to that, I always felt sorry for him and tried my best to take care of him when he needed it. Today, of course, I would have sought some professional help and support, for me as well as for him.

Once we were back in the UK in the early autumn of 1979, after George signed to play for Hibernian, I put my heart and soul into being the perfect wife again, even though that was doomed from the start because I was married to a far from perfect husband. Even His Lordship has admitted that he was a 'very bad' husband and that our marriage never stood a chance. Having said that, for every row or fight we had I can always think of at least two or three good things we did together. There were times when he would disappear for days, sure, but then when he reappeared he might take me on a shopping spree and be the best company you could wish for. One time George even bought me a fur coat as we were walking past a shop off the King's Road because he felt so guilty about coming home drunk the night before.

Maybe I've just been in denial, tried all my life with

George to put all the bad things to the back of my mind. I am certainly not denying that George and I had more than our fair share of ups and downs, because we did, but as I said, these moments were to my mind outweighed by the good times, and I always try to remember His Lordship as the man I fell in love with because that is how I want Calum to see him as well. Of course Calum is now old enough to know about the sort of man his dad was; I can't stop him from reading the newspapers, George's books, or this book in fact. He has even experienced the violence at first hand inside pubs when he has been to stay with his dad in England. But I want to visualise George as a great footballer and the sleek, toned, humorous man I loved.

His Lordship was an absolute angel for those first few weeks back in London. I had been so worried that the minute we landed he would head straight to Tramp, but I think he realised how important it was for him to make this new job at Hibernian work, especially when the press turned up in droves at the airport to meet us. The last few clubs he had played for in the United States had sacked him or given him the option to leave because of his outrageous, unmanageable behaviour. He would regularly miss training, turn up late to matches or go AWOL for days when a big match was scheduled, so when Hibernian offered him the chance to play back in the United Kingdom, His Lordship jumped at it. I hadn't seen him this excited about playing football for a long time. The American teams he had been playing against had featured the odd genius on a par with him – legendary players like Pele, Cruyff and Beckenbauer – but the standard generally was on the poor side and the experience was nothing like playing in a league back in Britain.

So we hit an almost serene interval. We spent our evenings together when he was not in Scotland training and would either go out to dinner or eat, just the two of us, in our flat in London. Even though His Lordship was playing in Scotland, I stayed in London near my family; after a match on the Saturday, George would fly down to be with me until mid-week, when he would have to go back for training. But I think perhaps the Hibernian people started to get a little nervous about George's behaviour in London because they soon asked me to go and live with him in Edinburgh. I said yes. We found a really lovely little apartment just outside the city and quickly grew to be very fond of our new home town. The locals seemed to accept us too, which is always important. I even got invited to open a safari park once on the outskirts of Edinburgh, and was photographed holding some beautiful lion and bear cubs (enjoyable despite the fact, uncaptured by the camera, that they peed all over me).

But the good times in Edinburgh were far too shortlived. Everything was calm and happy for a few months, but then just the slightest thing began to set George off again. I was wanting to start a family at the same time, and had already had one false alarm. One day when I was chatting to him about potential names for a baby, I mentioned one I liked and he went straight into the biggest sulk just because he didn't like it. It was a sign. He didn't actually storm off that night, but I knew things were brewing for an almighty bender. Lo and behold, a few nights later he got drunk and left me in a restaurant. I knew that when he got home he would be in a bad mood, and at best would verbally assault me, at worst . . . well. George always tried to goad me and push me away whenever he felt we were getting too close because he was so afraid of expressing his feelings. There were times when he would tell me (and it wasn't true, because I knew him too well) that he didn't love me just so he could go out.

Once again the familiar routine began to kick in. George started to miss training at Hibernian, and of course it wasn't long before they were forced into showing him the door. It was such a shame because everyone always showed willing to keep on giving George a chance, but there were limits and His Lordship always managed to reach them. Indeed, no matter how many times he messed up, if he upset one club, another would offer him a place in their side. Some of them obviously were not of the calibre of Manchester United, but they still wanted

George Best to play for them. He could easily have carried on his career in England and taken it to a new level if he'd taken advantage of those chances, instead of failing to repay the generosity and faith of the teams and people who believed in him enough to take a chance on him.

So George's drinking had cut short his time with yet another team. He was also getting fed up with all the attention being paid to his extra-time activities by certain British papers, and wanted out. But as usual George never said anything to me about his sacking, and as usual within days he had another job offer – back in California from the San Jose Earthquakes. So in the spring of 1980, just over half a year after we left Los Angeles, I found myself packing up all our belongings once more, this time to move to San Jose.

In a way, I was relieved. When we had returned to London I was delighted because I thought George would behave himself and that I would be close to my family in case anything went wrong. And things were great for a while, but as his Lordship's bad behaviour increased I actually found myself wishing to be back in Los Angeles with friends like Cher and Josephine. My mother was always wonderful and understanding about George and she always told the truth about how she felt about him, but I still felt lonely and just couldn't let her know how I was really feeling. At least when he disappeared in California I could pick up the phone and call Josephine or jump in the car and drive to Cher's house for a natter.

So, alongside the sadness I felt when my husband was fired yet again, I was secretly happy to be moving back to the place that to me had always felt like a real home.

13 Bottle or Baby?

'I finally caught up with George in one of the other bars on the beach. I sat down next to him – he was as drunk as a skunk and he smelt like a rat, I remember – took his hand and told him that I had something very important to tell him. "I'm pregnant, George." His Lordship's eyes lit up and he said "That's great!" – then turned back to his drink. He didn't hug me or kiss me, but I knew from those fleeting seconds after I'd first told him that he was as excited as I was.'

YOU WOULD HAVE thought that being sacked from one team just weeks before would have put George in a positive frame of mind for the fresh challenge of a new team, but that would have been far too sensible an approach. Instead, trouble came knocking the minute His Lordship's plane landed in San Jose.

George left London on Wednesday, 23 April 1980, leaving me tearful at the airport as he promised me that 'this time it will all work out'. It might have been St George's Day, but my George was no saint. When I called his hotel room the next day, there was no answer. In a panic I called John Carbury, the Earthquakes' manager, and found out that despite landing in San Jose George, instead of picking up his luggage and checking into his hotel, had immediately booked himself on a flight to Los Angeles. Not only had he snubbed the San Jose Earthquakes soccer team bosses, he'd even had the cheek to call them and tell them that he was going off to his bar. I phoned Bestie's for confirmation. Bobby McAlinden told me George had been drinking from the minute he got there.

I then called the Conservation of Manpower, an Alcoholics Anonymous-type organisation which offers people like me professional advice, and they told me that I should go and get him straight away. So I phoned again and told him to call Bobby and tell him not to let George drink any more. George had gone back to America to be given yet another chance, but the minute he got there he'd gone straight to Los Angeles and Bestie's – I just couldn't believe it. As soon as I heard I knew there was now no chance for him at all, and this feeling was confirmed when I called back several hours later and John told me that George had, unsurprisingly, failed to turn up for training. He'd also, therefore, missed the press conference set up to announce the fact that he was joining the team. In the end John went down to Los Angeles himself, collected George and brought him back to San Jose. Once he was where he should be, His Lordship called me. I was so fed up with him that I blurted out, 'I want a divorce!' Of course I didn't mean it, I just wanted to let him know how angry and upset I was with him. Water off a duck's back.

I flew out to San Jose a week later after tying up loose ends in the UK, and His Lordship was as good as gold for two weeks. Life, in fact, was bliss during that short time. George paid me lots of attention and spent every night at home. We were like a real couple. Then he flew down to Los Angeles to check up on Bestie's and that was the end of that. He was ever the slave to drink, and immediately started on what turned out to be a seven-day bender. As a result His Lordship missed his very first game with the Earthquakes. Why they didn't fire him there and then I don't know. I suppose they were willing to stick with him because he was George Best.

It was while George was on this bender that I found out that I was pregnant. Both of us wanted a family, and we'd talked about having children, but there had never seemed to be a right time actually to go for it. We were always on the move, from this club to that club, from this city to that city, even from country to country, so I was absolutely delighted to find out that I was pregnant. My first reaction was a desire to tell His Lordship, but of course he was down in Los Angeles nursing his beloved drink. Despite that, and without really thinking about it – I was just so excited by the news and was desperate to share it with my husband – I packed a bag and jumped on a plane.

I arrived at Bestie's in due course, but Bobby told me

George had left earlier so I spent the next hour looking for him. I finally caught up with him in one of the other bars on the beach. I sat down next to him – he was as drunk as a skunk and he smelt like a rat, I remember – took his hand and told him that I had something very important to tell him. 'I'm pregnant, George.' His Lordship's eyes lit up and he said 'That's great!' – then turned back to his drink. He didn't hug me or kiss me, but I knew from those fleeting seconds after I'd first told him that he was as excited as I was, that the trip had been worth it. I also knew that when he was on a bender nothing could tear him away from the bottle, not even the news that he was going to be a father. Still, I tried. 'Darling, you need to come home and sober up because you're going to be a dad.' He continued to show me how thrilled he was with the prospect, but the poor soul still had to say, 'I can't come home yet, I've got to finish this' – meaning his drinking session. As he picked up his glass again, I quietly left the bar.

I got in a taxi and went straight over to see Cher. When I told her I was pregnant, she couldn't have been happier for me. She invited me to stay with her for a while, so I spent a week at Cher's and we talked babies – she'd already had lots of experience with Elijah and Chastity. She told me, among lots of other advice, that I should be prepared to do it all alone. I assumed she was talking from experience, as Greg had a similar addiction to George's. When the week was up, and still with no sign of His Lordship, who was either still drinking or drying out somewhere, Cher and I decided we needed some fun, so we went to Las Vegas as at that time she was doing a show at Caesar's Palace. This trip to Las Vegas – and it could have been anywhere really – was a special one. I had the best time in the world there, and relished it more because I knew I wouldn't be able to go off and live it up like that again for a long time now that I would have to be responsible for another human being. I was with all my friends and people I worked with, and I had complete freedom to just hang out with them and watch the show I had helped with for many years. I will always remember this trip with fondness.

Still, you have to return to the real world some time, and when I returned to mine George was back, and he was soon fussing over me like the expectant father he was. Cher had told me that I would never feel the same again as I would during a pregnancy, but I hadn't believed her. But about three months into my pregnancy I realised that she was right. I had been so active, working out every day, running here, there and everywhere, but the doctors had advised me to start to take things very easy so all I could really do was sit at home and do needlepoint. I must say though that I loved being pregnant. It's a wonderful excuse to be self-indulgent and people treat you in a special way. I had an incredible sense of peace about me. Even though everything might not have been perfectly idyllic, you would never have known it from my demeanour. I was a happy girl, and that made for a happy baby.

His Lordship was back training with the team so he was not there during the days, and I was glad he was finally buckling down. I think the news that he was going to be a father had quickly sunk in and he was determined to be a good dad so he was trying as hard as he could to do things the right way. We even decided to buy our own house in San Jose, and in July 1980 we began looking for homes. Soon, however, the novelty – for George – of living a normal life wore off and he started to pick fights and would go into prolonged sulks. He would create an argument over nothing just so he could justify to himself going off on a bender.

At one point during this troublesome period I became so desperate for him to stay at home that I started putting sleeping pills in his tea without him knowing. I know it was probably not the right thing to do, and probably quite dangerous especially as George was an alcoholic, but it was the only way I could think of to keep him in the house. On one occasion I put three pills in his tea and he was so sick he couldn't even get out of bed. That scared me, and soon put a stop to my little tricks, even though George just thought he had a particularly bad hangover. He carried on picking fights over the tiniest thing, anything for an excuse to get out of the house and go drinking and then not feel guilty about it all, and to add to the pressure Graham Wright, who was sent to us by the publishers to help George with his autobiography *Where Do I Go From Here?*, came to stay. Most of the time George was not at home, either playing with the team or drinking, so there I was, with child and trying my best to accommodate Graham and his girlfriend.

Despite this, everything began to run smoothly again, and George, Lindy and I decided to go down to Los Angeles for a few days. George, of course, headed straight for Bestie's while Lindy and I went shopping. Later on we went to the bar to find him and I visited the bathroom. On the wall there I saw some crude graffiti: 'GB gives good head – I gave GB good head'. Underneath that someone else had written: 'So what, so has everyone else!' I laughed at first, but then I felt awful when I read it again, even though it didn't surprise me.

George had embarked on what turned out to be a two-day binge, which relatively speaking wasn't so bad. He had arranged to meet me at the bar for dinner on our last night in LA but he didn't show up, so we started trawling all the other bars nearby to find him. We must have looked a sight: a pregnant woman all dressed up and her sister looking for a drunk. By the time we eventually found George we had missed our flight back to San Jose. Of course it didn't help matters that I was pregnant and feeling very emotional – as I said, when what mattered was how long His Lordship's binges lasted, not if they happened at all, two days was pretty good for him.

About halfway through the pregnancy, I picked up and began to feel a lot better. My body was getting used to the changes, the hormones were settling down and slowly I began to feel more like my old self. In October 1980 we made a bid on a house, but we lost it to a cash buyer. Before we lost out, His Lordship took me furniture shopping and was behaving once more like a husband with responsibilities. Later that same month we put another bid in on a different house and got it. I was so excited that my family was finally starting to come together. It was a lovely little townhouse with a pool and a back garden which would be perfect for the baby. Also in October George signed a contract to play full time for the Earthquakes and began training hard. He had really set his mind on making it work this time, he told me (I know you're thinking 'I've heard that before'). I was happy, nearly six months into my term and filling up my days fixing up our new home, decorating, choosing furniture and everything else that we needed. George was playing a couple of away games during the move itself, so all he had to do when he came home was put his toothbrush in the holder and hang his clothes in the closet. I moved us, lock, stock and boxes.

George was only back for a few weeks when he had to go off again to Lake Tahoe with the team for a game and an after-match dinner. I was feeling, and looking, like the size of a house, so I chose not to travel; Lindy went in my place. Two days after they'd left George called to tell me he had been gambling and lost all of his money. I was devastated. I sat at home worrying, even though Lindy also called me and told me everything would be OK. His Lordship came home with his tail between his legs. He walked into the house and repeated the fact that he had no money and no presents for me because he'd lost it all in the casino. I was distraught, but about to tell him that it didn't really matter when he started pulling out wads of cash from his jacket and trouser pockets. In one pocket he had $1,600, in another pocket there was $1,000, and on it went. He was just pulling out money everywhere, laughing his head off, me grinning like the Cheshire Cat. (Later on, George did something similar with Mary Stavin, whom he was dating at the time, only on that occasion he spread all the money out on the bed. It became a famous story which most people have heard: the room-service waiter delivers champagne to the hotel room and, as he sees George lying on the bed with Mary surrounded by all the money, asks: 'Where did it all go wrong, Mr Best?') The next day we went furniture shopping again and spent all the money on things we needed for our home. At last His

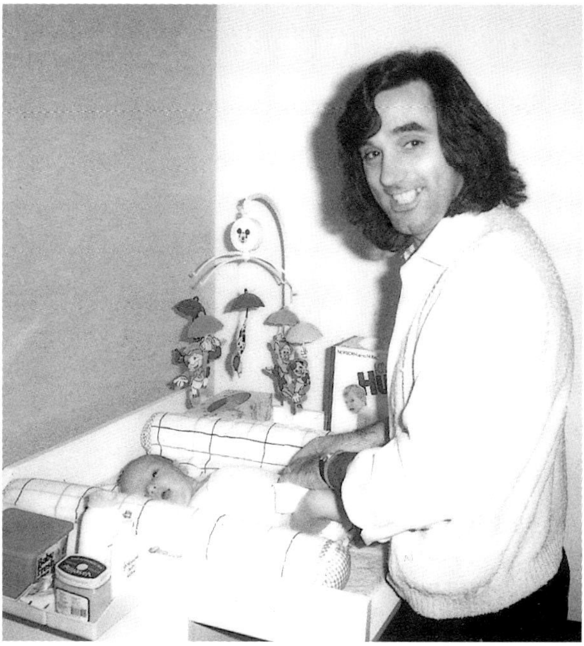

His Lordship playing with baby Calum.

Momentarily contented. (Bottom photograph © Eddie Sanderson)

Above George and Chris Dangerfield, team-mates at the San Jose Earthquakes, enjoy playing with their sons.

Right Calum looks the part in football kit and with San Jose Earthquakes ball, 1982.

Above Four generations of the Best family. From left to right: George's grandfather, Calum, George and George's father Dickie.

Right A rare happy Christmas, 1983.

With Hot Chocolate's Errol Brown and his wife at Tramp, 1985.

Left With Cynthia Payne in London in 1986.

Right A ridiculous dress, a ridiculous necklace and a ridiculous party but Nigel Dempster of the *Daily Mail* was nice to me in spite of everything.
(© Richard Young)

Below With Christopher Carajohn at the house in Marlow that he rented for me in 1987.

Left With Cher, her sister Georganne and the wig lady at the St James Club Hotel in London, 1988.

Below George and Calum in London, 1989.

Lordship was contributing constructively, and I had another of my 'everything really is going to be all right' moments.

At some point in those last months of 1980 George went to see a doctor about his drinking because the team had warned him he had to cut back if he wanted to stay on with them. The doctor gave him some pills called Antebuse which were supposed to make him sick if he took so much as a sip of alcohol. When he started to take them they were great; they actually stopped him from drinking because he had a fear of what might happen if he drank. Then he began to test the medicine to see how many actual sips of alcohol it would take before he was ill, and of course over time he built up such a resistance to the chemicals they hardly made any difference. At the time I didn't know he was doing this; whenever we went out for dinner he would order water or a soft drink. He only confessed later: on these occasions, every time he popped off to the toilet in a restaurant he would also sneak up to the bar and grab a drink. Then one night in the middle of his course of medication he came home and I could smell the booze on him. I was horrified by the thought that he was deliberately making himself ill just so he could have another drink, but it didn't seem to matter to George.

His Lordship saw it as something of a game, one that he desperately wanted to win. There were times when he would only take half a pill and go off and have just a few drinks. He also used to hold them in his mouth, take them out afterwards and put them in the pocket of his jeans when I wasn't looking, which was a silly thing to do really because I would always check his pockets before I did the laundry. He knew that, and I think getting caught every now and then was part of the game. He would drive me crazy with these sorts of tricks. The pills were for his benefit, but he still couldn't summon up enough of a sense of responsibility to take them. It got to the stage where I used to make him sit down and show me that he had taken them – it was like getting a child to take medicine. Even then he would sometimes stick the pill in a small gap between his teeth so that when he opened his mouth I would think that he had swallowed it.

It was soon obvious that the pills were not going to work. It was only after we had separated that George took any drastic action (other than the odd stay at a rehabilitation centre or attendance at Alcoholics Anonymous) in his bid to become sober – by having an operation. The procedure involved having about a dozen pellets implanted in his stomach. These pellets would slowly dissolve over the course of a year releasing certain chemicals into his body, the idea being a similar one to the pills: their presence would make him feel violently ill after just one drink. At the time this operation was an incredibly dangerous one and George had to travel to Sweden to have it done because just about every surgeon in Britain refused. And after it had been done His Lordship just went out and did exactly the same as he had with the pills: he probed the pellets' limits with alcohol. When the first lot of pellets dissolved a few years later he had it done again, but this second operation went horribly wrong and he was left in agonising pain. The slit in his stomach lining got infected and the pellets started to fall out. George later revealed that the doctor had for some reason refused to stitch him back up and he finally had to go to a plastic surgeon to have the damage repaired. He was left with a permanent scar as a result of this, and from that day on he vowed to deal with his drinking his own way – which of course meant, at best, thinking about the problem over a glass of champagne.

With George largely off the drink towards the end of 1980, he needed something else to fill up his time. He was determined to steer clear of bars so that he wouldn't be tempted, which meant he was at the house a lot when there were no training sessions. He tried taking up golf because he thought it would be relaxing, so I bought him a set of golf clubs, even though he only ever used the three-iron and the putter on his way round a course. He really enjoyed the sport and became quite a good golfer, even with just two clubs, but then the boys started playing as well. Even though they were not in a bar, there was still the same clubbable atmosphere, and some of them, with their usual lack of consideration, would openly drink between holes and then meet up at the clubhouse at the end. So His Lordship ending up having a few drinks while he played. To his credit, when that started to happen he gave up the game, which was a good thing because he was getting into some sticky situations.

I remember one occasion when we were supposed to do a photo shoot for one of the newspapers which was running a story about my pregnancy and what a happy family we now were. George was playing golf, so we agreed with the photographer to do the shoot at the clubhouse. Well, I arrived to find George looking all red and blotchy and I knew straight away that he had been drinking because the medication would make his face break out into a rash if he drank. I asked one of the boys if he had had a drink and he told me, 'Oh, Bestie popped into the bar for a quick one between holes. He's fine though.' It turned out that 'a quick one' had been two shots of vodka and a six pack of beer. His face looked so terrible that the photographer ended up shooting the pictures in black and white, which made him look not quite as awful.

So, what to do now? Well, His Lordship has always been artistic and creative. In fact, people have never really had the opportunity to discover how talented George is with his poetry and drawings. He never really had the sort of education which would have allowed him to express himself to the full in this way, but when he set his mind to it he could paint or write very well indeed. So when he said he wanted to paint a mural in the nursery we had set up for our son, I was delighted. For two weeks His Lordship worked on this mural. He drew it totally free-hand and it featured the Disney characters the Lady and the Tramp, which he referred to as Mummy and Daddy, with a huge rainbow in the background. He was so proud of that wall, and I was so proud of him. He was still taking his pills (just), staying out of the bars and being a great husband.

But in December 1980 George had a major setback. The

Earthquakes lost a match by the incredible scoreline 10–7, and he was mad. George had scored three goals and weighed in with three assists, but the team was just not strong enough to hold on. After this disastrous result – has any team ever scored seven and lost? – all he wanted to do was have a drink, and he came home later several sheets to the wind. I was not too happy as I was nearly eight months' pregnant by this time, but at least there was a reason for it. What bothered me much more was that after that he kept up the drinking. He had had such good intentions and I thought that finally he was on the road to sobriety, but just one session with the stuff had set him off again and he started to come in later and later, just like old times.

Then, in January 1981, George had such a bad scare that it shook him into getting counselling. I was just a couple of weeks away from my due date when George was pulled in for drink driving. That was the last thing I needed on my plate. He called me from the station after the police arrested him. They had pulled him over in his car because they had seen him weaving all over the road. His Lordship begged me to come and collect him but I was so angry with him that I let him stew overnight behind bars. I thought a night in the drunks tank might do him some good. But when I told him he could stay right where he was, he got so angry I just hung up. He eventually came home at nine the following morning when they let him out. He was as miserable as sin and just wanted to sleep. I was relieved that he'd come straight home and relieved that he was tired, so it seemed my ploy had worked.

Five days later George checked into therapy, thanks to his manager, John Carbury. His Lordship had decided again that he wanted to make a real effort to get sober, but it was John who pushed him in the right direction and offered to help out with financing and finding a suitable place. George went to his first class on 19 January, but when he came home all he could talk about was how much he had hated it. For some reason he didn't like the people there, whom I think reminded him too much of himself. He did say he would try to find somewhere else to go, but it would be another month before he again checked into the rehab clinic. In the meantime, our son came into the world.

14 The Reason

'One night His Lordship got up because he was restless and decided to look in on Calum. It was lucky that he did, because it probably saved Calum's life. George found his son standing up in his cot, trying to cry but not able to make a sound. He immediately scooped up Calum in his arms and came charging into the bedroom to tell me that we were going to the hospital straight away.'

At 11 P.M. on 5 February 1981, I went into labour. His Lordship was out drinking. I called him at the Lancashire Hot Pot pub and told him I needed to go to the hospital. He was a bit put out because he was in the middle of a game of darts at the time, but he dutifully drove home, picked me up, and off we went to the hospital. I had been having contractions all day and was feeling very peculiar. I had passed some of the time planting jasmine trees in the front garden, which probably didn't help matters, although I later came to learn my actions were connected with a phenomenon called 'nesting'.

We arrived in one piece, and George immediately began to feel panicky, mainly because he just didn't know what to do with himself. The doctors were wonderful, though. They gave me a thorough examination but sent me home and told me to come back the next day because I was only three centimetres dilated. It was a false alarm. His Lordship drove me home and we got into bed, but within the hour I knew that I was definitely in labour this time and I woke George up to take me back to the hospital.

I had a hard time of it, but George was just wonderful. He kissed me, cuddled me and made me do my breathing because the pain was really bad. He stayed with me all through the night in the delivery room, comforting me through what was a miserable and very painful natural birth. I don't care what other women say about the wonders of birth, for me it was horrendous. The end result was wonderful of course, but the actual process was not at all pleasant. We had been to a couple of La Marrs pre-natal classes and even now I'm surprised I managed to get His Lordship to go along. We knew how to breathe, and George knew how to encourage me to do it properly, but it did me absolutely no good at all! Finally, at 7.02 a.m. on 6 February, our beautiful son Calum Milan Best was born.

The umbilical cord was wrapped around Calum's neck when he emerged, and for a minute or so things were touch and go, but His Lordship saved the day when the doctor asked him to cut it. He took the scissors and proudly cut the cord before bursting into tears. There was my macho husband, in delivery-room scrubs, crying his eyes out as he picked up his newborn son. It was a wonderfully happy image that will stay with me for ever.

After the exhilaration of giving birth had worn off, I became worried as I was very weak due to loss of blood. The doctors recommended that I have a transfusion, which became a source of some anxiety for me five years later when the hospital wrote to me and said I should have an AIDS test. I could hardly think straight, but I went to the hospital and had the test right away. I am A positive, which is quite a rare type of blood, so the hospital was able positively to track down the source of the blood I had been given. As it turned out I was in the clear, but waiting for the results was the most frightening time of my life.

George was so proud of his new son, and impressed with the perfect timing of his coming into the world. Calum was born at two minutes past seven in the morning on the West Coast of America, which meant that it was 3.02 p.m. in Britain. This was the exact moment when the Munich air disaster happened back in 1958, which sadly killed many of the Manchester United Busby Babes. George was thrilled that his son was born at the same time on the same date.

Three days after I gave birth the hospital finally let me go home, and I then had to get used to the task of having to change nappies and feed Calum in the middle of the night. Those first few months were hard, but I wouldn't have changed it for anything in the world. I was so happy. His Lordship was too, even though you couldn't get him anywhere near a nappy! He was like most new fathers: he loved to pick up the baby and cuddle him, sing him to sleep or tell him stories, but the minute there was a whiff in the air he was nowhere to be found! Coping with everything to do with bringing up and looking after a baby made me very independent; I even carried on paying all the bills as George was always useless when it came to money. He hadn't known anything about managing his own life when I first met him – he'd left home for United at such a young age and was looked after by the club for the next decade or so, had everything done for him so that he didn't have to worry about it and could concentrate on playing football. After we were married, I had taken over that management role. So there I was in my first weeks home from the hospital trying to sort out bills, clean up the house and look after Calum and my husband. Needless to say, it made me very tired. His Lordship was still celebrating, down at the bar handing out cigars.

In fact, those first couple of weeks at home with Calum, His Lordship went out every night, even though he never came back too drunk. Partly, I think, it was comfortable routine, but also he just wanted to get out because being a father was a frightening idea; OK in small chunks, but not 24 hours a day. My parents came over to stay, as proud grandparents do, but as soon as they arrived George started to come home a little more worse for wear. My mother, bless her, didn't really understand what was going on. She used to ask me why George would go out and not come home until the following morning. I felt bad for my parents as I didn't really have an answer for them, but I had no time to feel bad for myself, even though I was stuck in the middle of this problem. One day towards the end of February George came home at half-past seven in the morning and said he had gotten so drunk he had fallen asleep in his car. It was a minor offence in the catalogue of George incidents, so I put it straight out of my mind and concentrated on enjoying my time with my parents before they flew back home a few days later.

George carried on mostly staying out of our way, until he came home to tell me that he was over his latest binge and had agreed to meet again with John Carbury to discuss treatment for his problem. He knew the pills were not working because he could not trust himself to take them, and he'd finally realised that he needed the discipline of a live-in centre where counsellors could keep an eye on him and encourage him. John, of course, was well aware that George needed help, and took a proactive view on the matter. He had tried many times to sit George down after matches and talk to him, but His Lordship always rebuffed him. On one occasion when George was out drinking with the team John tried to get him to stop, and George scarpered. Another time, John tracked him down to Bestie's and took him back to Bobby's flat, where George used to stay when he went down to Los Angeles. On yet another occasion, when John actually got George to sit down for a chat, he offered His Lordship a cup of tea, but George insisted on making it himself and wandered off into the kitchen. John waited in the living room for about five minutes but heard nothing. He got the shock of his life when he went into the kitchen and realised that His Lordship had managed to squeeze through the tiniest window in the world to escape – and all because he wanted another drink. But during this latest meeting John did finally manage to get through to him, and on Monday, 2 March George checked into an in-patient rehab centre.

I was so relieved that George was finally taking the steps himself to find a cure for his problem. My parents had gone home and George was in the clinic, so Calum, Dallas and myself had the prospect of a few weeks to ourselves at home. But as usual it was all too good to be true. Just days after George entered the rehab clinic, the police knocked on my door. I invited the officer in and he stood there in my living room and told me that the night ten days or so before when George said he had slept in his car, a girl who lived across the street had accused him of attempting to rape her. This young girl said that His Lordship broke into her house and when she opened her eyes he was standing over her looking at her. She said he didn't do anything, but she called the police straight away. George later vehemently denied that he had done it, and I believed him, but I was still mortified that he could be accused of something like that. This teenage girl had accused my husband of breaking and entering and attempted rape, and there was nothing I could do about it. I was in such a state. I had a month-old baby, my husband was a drunk and all I could think was, 'What else can possibly happen to me?'

I didn't speak to George about it at the time because he was in the clinic trying to get well and the last thing I wanted to do was upset him or push him into a relapse. All I wanted was for him to get well so that we could live like a normal family. I knew that while I was having a hard time coping with all of this, George was not having much more fun in rehab. When his due date to leave arrived, the doctors decided he needed to stay for a bit longer. They labelled him 'dishonest and superficial' and therefore he needed to carry on with the counselling and treatment. For once, George did as he was told and stayed in the hospital before being allowed home at the end of March.

His Lordship then got to know about the accusation against him, and he went to see the police to sort everything out. George readily admitted that he couldn't have found his way into his own house that night in the state he was in, let alone anyone else's, and the police admitted to George that the description the girl had given of the intruder did not fit George at all, it was nothing like him. In the end he wasn't charged, and I can't tell you what a sense of relief washed over me – over both of us, in fact. There was no evidence whatsoever to link George to the alleged crime, and the matter was dropped.

George didn't talk about his experiences at the clinic all that much, but I knew that he had hated it because he used to refer to the place as 'the prison'. He later wrote in his autobiography that he knew he would be back on the drink within twelve months because he had learnt how to give the counsellors the answers they wanted to hear. He was absolutely right when he said 'Drunks are great liars and conmen', and the doctors had been absolutely right to call him 'dishonest'. George had effectively conned the hospital into declaring he had a 'clean bill of health', although he had promised himself he would remain dry for one year. He had every intention of picking up a glass again in the future, but when he was discharged I believed the treatment had worked wonders.

His Lordship was certainly in a great mood when he came home. For the first time ever he was house-proud, baby-proud, even wife-proud! George even changed a few nappies in those first few weeks and attended bathtimes and bedtimes, which he loved to do, but apart from that I still did all the housework, cooking and washing, it was still me who got up in the middle of the night to feed Calum, and His Lordship still expected his dinner to be on the table and his clothes hanging in the wardrobe ready to wear – like a lot of men, I suppose! And I was more than happy to do that; I was just so delighted that we were finally together, acting like a real family. It was wonderful to see him this way, wonderful to be with him, although I didn't get too excited. I suspected he was a 'new man' only in the sense that he might now moderate his drinking, not give it up altogether, and with that always came the possibility of a relapse. Having said that, I was just so happy that His Lordship was for now off the drink and that he was spending time with his son.

Then one night in May George went off to the bar. I sat at home fearing he would start drinking again, but to my relief he came home sober as a judge. In fact, I wasn't just relieved, I was ecstatic. Everything continued to run smoothly for months; His Lordship was truly like a different man and we had a nice peaceful life. I kept thinking that at any moment he would fall off the wagon, but to his credit George kept to his word and I began to trust him again. It finally seemed as if George had turned his life around and was serious about staying clean, sober and out of trouble.

During this golden period His Lordship started to live and breathe football again. When training was on he would do his stuff and then spend the rest of the day with the younger players, sharing his knowledge of the game with them. These youngsters were, needless to say, completely in awe of him and would spend hours hanging off his every word as he showed them new moves and skills. George would also put aside time to talk about the game, and he really began to feel as if he was making a difference, which did wonders for his self-esteem. It is such a shame that he never became a football coach because he was such a natural at it.

Two months passed, three months, four, five, then six. I was on top of the world. We even went to Las Vegas to see Cher in concert and George resisted the many and varied temptations to drink and gamble there. I thought that if he could behave himself in the most sinful city in the world, he could behave himself anywhere. I really believed he had cracked it, especially when he made it through two traumatic incidents in September and October without reaching for the bottle.

Early in September we flew home to England as George had agreed to play in a testimonial match. I will never forget that flight. Because we didn't have a bank account in England at that time and no credit cards, we had a large amount of cash with us, about £2,000, and it had been agreed that I would be responsible for it. I was also responsible for the baby, of course, so when I went to the bathroom to change Calum's nappy, I brought everything with me and put it down on the sink. As I left I picked the stuff back up, but managed to leave the cash, which was in a nappy bag, behind. When I realised my mistake I was already back in my seat. I rushed back to the bathroom, but it was too late: the money had gone. I immediately told the flight attendants, who informed the police, so when we landed in London everybody had to sit in their seats while the police came slowly up the aisle, searching for the cash. George was furious with me for losing the money, and I was furious with him because he had slept through the whole flight and left me with all the work. The money wasn't found, and everybody was allowed to leave the plane. Thankfully, the airline called us a few days later to say that the cash had been found. It appeared that somebody had panicked and shoved it hard down the side of their seat.

After the testimonial, His Lordship went gambling with some of the guys. I waited in the hotel, dreading the moment when he would come home drunk. I seriously thought that if His Lordship was to fall off the wagon, London would be the place, but he didn't. When he got back, he was fine. Everything was rosy again, and we went off to Belfast so that His Lordship could show his son off to his family and do some work with handicapped kids. The whole time we were there George never once mentioned drinking; he didn't even so much as look at a pub if we drove past one.

I genuinely felt my husband was cured, especially when the traumatic scare of Calum being rushed into hospital in San Jose the next month didn't send him over the edge either. Calum, who at eight months was just starting to take his first steps, started wheezing one day, but when I took him to the doctor I was told not to worry, that everything would be fine. That same night His Lordship got up because he was restless and decided to look in on Calum. It was lucky that he did, because it probably saved Calum's life. George found his son standing up in his cot, trying to cry but not able to make a sound. He immediately scooped up Calum in his arms and came charging into the bedroom to tell me that we were going to the hospital straight away.

I was terrified that Calum was going to die. His face was all red and he could hardly breathe. When we arrived at the hospital the doctors immediately put him in an oxygen tent and then told us that he had croup, an inflammation of the larynx which makes breathing very difficult. It really was touch and go for a while, and if His Lordship hadn't found him when he did, our beautiful son might not be here today. To this day George is so grateful that he was sober at the time.

Calum was in the hospital for just over a week, his worried parents climbing the walls at home, before the doctors gave him the all-clear. After a scare like that I felt too frightened to let him sleep in a room on his own, but the hospital gave us a special humidifier that we could put in Calum's room which helped break down the congestion in his lungs. The episode brought us even closer together as a family. George was there for me, which is just what I needed at that time. The fact that he hadn't touched a drop of drink during that stressful time made me certain that George was finally the man I'd always known he could be.

His Lordship had been dry for nearly nine months when suddenly it all went horribly wrong. What made it worse when it happened was that there was just no rhyme or reason to it. He had had a break in Las Vegas without a relapse, had managed to survive Calum's brush with death without reaching for the booze and had been in several bars without so much as a hint of a problem. Which is why I had no reason in the world to stop him going to the races in Los Angeles at the end of November.

When he didn't call me, and as the hours stretched into days, I began to think the worst. I knew deep down in the pit of my stomach that he was back on the drink. I was devastated. George had been so good and now it appeared he had thrown it all away. I just couldn't track him down – the familiar story. On the second day I called Bestie's and Bobby told me that George was there, drunk. I didn't want to speak to him so I hung up, went into the bedroom and, more out of an overwhelming sense of disappointment than anger, began packing a case. I was mortified that he had gone back on the booze, and I wanted to put every thought of it out of my mind, which at that time for me meant a break from George and our home. So I put Calum and our suitcases in the car, picked up my friend Josephine and set off for her best friend Julie's house in Palm Springs.

Now, I'm not usually a fast driver, but I must have been speeding on this particular day because I soon saw flashing lights in my rearview mirror. After being pulled over, a very nice young policeman approached the car and asked to see my licence. When he saw the name, he said, 'You're not related to Georgie Best the soccer player, are you?' Straight away I knew that he was not going to give me a ticket. Indeed, he spent the next ten minutes telling me how wonderful George was and how he used to play football and watch every Aztecs game – and then handed me a ticket. Josephine thought this was hysterical, but I didn't. I was very much not in the mood.

Palm Springs was a haven for me. I just lay in the sun, played with Calum and tried to forget that I had a husband. It was just too sad to think that George had chucked the towel in again, effectively chosen the bottle over his family. We were all getting on so well! It was heartbreaking, and this was the first time that I said to myself that when it came down to it, I would always put Calum's welfare before George's.

I don't know why he started drinking again after those nine clean months. It was the longest time he had been dry since he first put a glass to his lips, but I suppose he just needed a drink, like all alcoholics. I desperately tried not to think about it. I didn't want to dwell on the unkept promises, all that good work wasted, but mainly I was trying to block out all the dark thoughts about what I knew was waiting for us round the corner.

15 I Think It's All Over . . .

'No matter where he went or what city he was in, people always bought George drinks because of who he was. It wasn't essential for George to be loaded when he walked into a pub intent on a session. He could walk into a bar with no money in his pockets, stay there for eight hours and still come home drunk. People thought they were doing him a favour by buying him a drink when it would have been far kinder to simply wish him a good afternoon.'

GEORGE ENDED 1981 and began 1982 on a bender. He'd had everything to look forward to in his life, but in the end he just couldn't see past the end of a glass. He was spending most of his nights now staggering home and either passing out or throwing up on the sofa (furniture never did last very long in our house). The drinking was taking over his life again and he was beginning to miss training and matches. One night he did come home at 2.30 a.m., but that was only because two people I had never seen before helped him to the front door. Of course I tried to talk to him, to reason with him, but to no avail.

I had been so proud of my husband when he was dry, and the nine months between the beginning of March and the end of November 1981 had been the happiest of my life. Now he just wanted to throw it all away. He began again to come back from bars with girls' phone numbers in his pockets, something that hadn't happened in a long time. I knew he had these numbers because he used to show me; George was never one for hiding things like that. When he came in, drunk as a lord, he would throw the numbers on the coffee table or pull them out of his pocket and wave them in front of my face. He always wanted me to see them. It was as if he was trying to prove that women still found him irresistible no matter what state he was in.

By the second week of January 1982 I was at my wits' end. I called George's counsellor in a fit of desperation because I didn't know what else to do, but he said he couldn't do anything. It was up to George to stop and no one else could make him do it. By this stage George was resorting to stealing money to get his next drink. As I said, I was responsible for all our money and paying the bills as George didn't have a clue when it came to things like that, so naturally I was trying to restrict the amount of money he had in his pocket at any one time in the hope that this would at least help to control the amount of alcohol he was putting away. But George just took to taking money straight out of my purse when I wasn't looking, and then resorted to stealing all the 25-cent coins, or quarters, I collected. This behaviour was especially sad because His Lordship didn't really have to steal to get a drink. No matter where he went or what city he was in, people always bought George drinks because of who he was. It wasn't essential for George to be loaded when he walked into a pub intent on a session. He could walk into a bar with no money in his pockets, stay there for eight hours and still come home drunk. People thought they were doing him a favour by buying him a drink when it would have been far kinder to simply wish him a good afternoon.

I remember once in Florida in 1979, when George was playing for the Fort Lauderdale Strikers, my sister and I were at home without any money, waiting for George to come back so we could go out for dinner. Hour after hour passed, then finally his car pulled up. But to our surprise he jumped out of his car, straight into my jeep and took off. Lindy and I looked at each other in shock and decided we would go out anyway. But when we got into George's car we saw that the petrol tank was empty, so we had to walk to the nearest bank to get some money wired over to me from the football club just so we could buy some petrol and get something to eat. George, of course, had taken all the cash out of my purse earlier that day.

Luckily I was not the only one worried about George. On 13 January John Carbury and another guy from the Earthquakes arrived at the house. I thought they had come to sack George and was beside myself with worry trying to figure out how we were going to survive without an income. Instead, John just looked at me and said, 'We're taking him back to the hospital.' At four o'clock that afternoon they frogmarched George to their car and drove him back to the hospital where he had first been treated. I carried on as though I hardly had a care in the world. On the inside I was in turmoil, but I tried to convince myself that I could carry on without him, for my and my son's sake. I suppose I was trying to shut it all out. I went to Santa Cruz, I went shopping and I spent my time keeping Calum occupied, as though George didn't exist at all.

I was unhappy, though. I still felt as though George, being back in hospital, was making me pay too high a price. Even though I was going out and doing things, I couldn't really enjoy them because so recently I'd been doing them with him, as a family, and I knew now that at the same time he was having a bad experience sweating everything out in the clinic. As much as I hate to admit it now, it was as if George had control over my emotions, even from a distance. I really did try to block George's existence from my mind, but it proved very difficult, especially when the hospital called me a few days after he checked in and told me they wanted me to visit him and take part in one of the counselling sessions. This put me in a foul mood because I was planning to take Calum to Palm Springs for a few days and I really didn't want to go and see him, to get involved with that side of things. But I felt twinges of guilt because George had accused me of not supporting him by going to his meetings last time he was in rehab, and he would bring the point up during arguments as the reason why he couldn't stay off the bottle (he always had to find someone else to blame; things were never George's fault).

Our fourth wedding anniversary came and went with me at home on my own chewing my fingernails and George sitting in a semi-circle with a group of strangers, baring their souls. George was now telling me that he did not want me to be there, so when the hospital next rang I refused again to go to the counselling sessions. I think George was just too embarrassed being back in the clinic to face me, was feeling the guilt that comes with the drying-out process. And I read in one of his books another possible reason: maybe it was because he was having an affair with one of his counsellors. Whatever the truth of the matter, I was at the end of my tether. Around the time of Calum's first birthday, early in February, I told George over the telephone that I wanted a divorce.

On Sunday, 12 February George was released from the hospital, but I had mixed feelings. I was happy that he had put himself through treatment again, but I couldn't bring myself to care enough this time and really didn't want him around. Don't get me wrong: I still loved him, but I'd been through all this 'I'm cured' stuff before and I was nervous of him and scared of his behaviour. I didn't know whether he was going to come home all lovey-dovey once more or head straight for a bar. As it turned out, he came home, but unlike just under a year before when he'd been so happy and pleased with himself after rehab, this time he was like a bear with a sore head.

A few weeks later he flew off to London to play in a testimonial match, which was definitely not the best place for him to be at that delicate time. While he was gone, I was the one who started the health kick. I began to jog, swim and play tennis every day, both to keep fit and to keep my mind off my husband. I *had* to occupy myself so that I wouldn't dwell on what His Lordship was doing in England. When he arrived back in town and I went to pick him up from the airport, I could smell the booze on him. It was not bad, but it was strong enough for me to notice. Three days later George sat me down and told me he was going to start attending Alcoholics Anonymous meetings because he desperately needed the support to stay sober. This time I offered to go with him, but he assured me he would find it easier if he went on his own. Again, I was delighted that he was taking his own steps to clean up again instead of being pushed by me or John Carbury, but a few days later, when George had told me he was at an AA meeting, someone else told me he had been to a bar instead. I was really cross with him over that, but I knew that getting cross with George never solved anything. So I calmed down quickly and left him to it.

I hadn't been joking when I asked George for a divorce. I had already made up my mind that I was leaving him. The real turning point was that notorious incident in February when I nearly ran over my husband after mistaking him for a tramp. Seeing George like that, I finally realised what really I had known all along, that George was a bigger baby than my one-year-old son and needed much more care than Calum. I just didn't have the strength to look after both of them, and I had always said that when crunch-time came, Calum would always come first. When I look back now, I know I made the right decision.

Those feelings, however, didn't stop me getting angry with the *Daily Star* newspaper early in March when one of their reporters called me at home from London to say they had a document proving that George and I had separated and that they were going to run the story. I knew there were no such documents anywhere. I had asked George for a divorce during a private telephone call (although he was drunk at the time and, I suspect, had not taken it seriously, or had completely forgotten about it), and even though I had decided to leave him George was totally unaware of my plans. But it's always possible, I suppose, that His Lordship had made his own plans after that phone conversation – that we will never know, but anyway, I had no intention of either him or me finding out anything from a newspaper. The *Daily Star* never did run the story, which pretty much proves they were just trying their luck.

I carried on with my plans, and started to look for a house to rent. George was totally unaware of the steps I was taking to sever our links because he was either in a drunken stupor or asleep. On 18 March he began one of his longest ever benders (it lasted twelve days in total). He had been out drinking that night at a banquet being held in honour of the New York Cosmos, who were in town to play the Earthquakes. Prior to that he had been trying to stay sober again and had managed it for about a week, but the banquet set him off again in a big way. Franz Beckenbauer and Pele were at the dinner and were on hand to celebrate the Budweiser Goal of the Year, which had been scored by none other than His Lordship. After the goal was shown everyone went up to George and congratulated him. Pele, considered by a lot of people the world's best ever player, also went over to George and told him, 'You are the greatest player in the world.' Well, His Lordship was over the moon with that, and started working his way round the room asking anyone who would listen, 'Do you want to go out and celebrate?' They all kept turning him down because they had the match to play the following day, but George, on a high, was determined and finally found someone to go out with.

It was, of course, just an excuse to drink. It didn't matter whether people said good things or bad things about him, George just wanted to drink. He did not have to, he chose to. He came home just before dawn the next day and threw up everywhere. A few short hours later he was off again. He missed the game against the Cosmos because he was still drinking.

I continued my quest for my own place to live. During this time Calum and I were of course still living in the family home, and every now and then we'd come across George in a terrible state. When his twelve-day binge ended I nursed him because he was having such awful withdrawals. He was shaking and sweating, couldn't keep anything down, and certainly couldn't get himself out of bed. He was as sick as a dog; I *had* to look after him. But even these withdrawals, which were on occasion so bad that George experienced hallucinations and thought he was literally dying, were not enough to stop him. Just days later he was back on the booze and missed another two games for the Earthquakes. John Carbury finally came to the end of his tether too and booted George off the team. I was amazed that he'd put up with His Lordship's antics for so long.

To add to the troubles, the teenage girl across the street, who had already falsely claimed that George had broken into her house and tried to rape her, now complained to me that George had exposed himself in front of her baby's window. I had no idea whether or not she was telling the truth, but her track record wasn't exactly sparkling so I denied it and told her to stop making things up about my husband. For all I knew George could have been doing these things, but the fact remained that when he was really drunk it was all he could do just to stagger home and make the couch. I began to feel even more hemmed in, that every time someone opened his or her mouth it was to say something bad about George. I took comfort in Calum and Dallas as George flew to London to put out feelers about playing over there again.

I just don't know what I would have done had I not had Calum and Dallas – but in mid-April that was to change suddenly too. I was walking to the postbox at the side of the road with Dallas trotting along beside me when this little dog from across the street came running over, yapping all the way, and began jumping all over Dallas. At first he took no notice of this tiny dog, until it began nipping at him, so Dallas barked back as if to warn it off. The little dog continued to harass Dallas, so Dallas chased it across the road towards its house. As I was calling him back, the owner came running out with a gun and shot Dallas right in front of me. I felt like one of my arms had been ripped off. I just couldn't believe what had just happened. I ran back to my house and called the police. They were sympathetic, but said there was nothing they could do because Dallas was on this man's property at the time. I was heartbroken. Dallas was OK finally but had a bullet in his shoulder which came to the surface years later. Then my sister Lindy took him to the vet to have it removed, brought him home, gave him some water and because it was so soon after the surgery, he died. The vet neglected to tell her that Dallas should not have been given any food or water for 24 hours. My sister sued that vet!

George returned home a few days later, but was more interested in getting to a bar than comforting me over Dallas's tragic death. We had a big showdown, and I asked him to leave. I told him to pack up his things and left the house for a while, but when I returned I saw that George hadn't taken the news too well. He had put a knife through one of his football pictures, thrown a football boot at the mirror and broken Calum's money box. He had also left our dressing gowns on the bed with four photographs of the two of us together scattered over them, along with a note saying how much he loved us both. I had no idea where he had gone or what he was doing, although I doubted he'd left for good, but at that point I didn't really care. All I felt was a huge weight lifted from my shoulders. I was proud that I'd had the power finally to carry out my wish to separate from George, to put myself and Calum first.

George called me the next day full of concern. He told me he was still having withdrawals but added that as soon as he got some cash together, he would send me some. I didn't believe him. I had already admitted to myself that he would never change. It was a difficult thing to do, because on the one hand I felt a failure that I hadn't managed to help him conquer the booze, and on the other I felt a failure for allowing our marriage to dissolve. But there you have it. I tried my very best.

On the last day of April, George, who was back at the house briefly, was officially served with the divorce papers. I told him that I still loved him, but only when he was sober, and the sad fact was that these days he was more often drunk, and I knew that would never change. George's reaction to all of this was to go out until four in the morning and get steaming drunk. It was a little awkward, to say the least, still to be sharing the same space with George after the papers had been served, but it was only for a few days because on 3 May I took him to the airport and he boarded a plane for London. We had actually managed to sit down and talk calmly about our respective futures, and George admitted he wanted to move back to

London. I agreed with him. Even though I was leaving him, I still wanted him to be as happy as he could be. I suggested that he stay with my mother while he found somewhere more permanent. Meanwhile, I would stay behind in San Jose with Calum for some breathing space and to sort things out before eventually moving back to England myself so that George could be nearer his son and still have a hand in his growing up, which I very much wanted for George's and Calum's sake.

Then, just two days after George had flown back to England, I was served some papers of my own, of the foreclosure variety. I stood there with them in my hands, in a state of shock. It turned out that the mortgage had not been paid and the bank was repossessing the house. Unbeknown to me, George had been taking money out of our account for the past several months so there had not been enough to cover the mortgage payments. After the initial shock wore off, something inside me snapped, and I moved another step away from dutiful wife and mother trying to do the right thing by everyone concerned to a new all-seeing and all-knowing woman. I was just a matter of weeks shy of my thirtieth birthday, and I decided once and for all not to let anything get me down any more. My beloved Dallas had been tragically killed, my marriage had just broken up and my house was being taken away from me; if anyone had met me that day, they would not have recognised me.

I threw myself into my new life. I went horse riding, played tennis, had a facial and had my nails done all on the first day. I was so focused on proving to myself that I was a new woman, that I could survive without George, and it certainly worked for me, so much so that I would recommend that approach to any woman going through a separation or divorce. Show everyone that you can cope, that *you* are the most important person in your own life. Do not wallow in self-pity; instead, think of all the great times you have had. I might have had some terrible times with George, but there were also wonderful times I wouldn't swap for anything in the world. Of course on occasions over the coming months I felt down, and there were some days when all I wanted to do was stay in bed and sleep, but I forced myself to get up and put on that happy face. I did not want Calum to pick up any bad vibes, to which young children are so susceptible. Also, I knew where I wanted to go in life now, and I made myself take that road, no matter how hard it was.

Part of that process of boosting my confidence, of doing something solely for me after years of looking after George, then Calum, was my decision to have breast implants. Many women pooh-pooh the idea of cosmetic surgery, but it really helped me get back on my feet. I needed to believe and have faith in myself at that stage in my life, and part of that, for me, came from my looks. To some that may seem shallow, but there isn't one person on the face of the earth who doesn't feel better about themselves when they are looking their best. I was feeling dowdy and tired after looking after Calum practically on my own for well over a year, and since his birth and six months of breast feeding my body had not zipped back into the shape it had been before. So, after ditching the excess baggage, I happily added on those few extra pounds. Now I felt even more able to stride out to face the world once again. And I would need every ounce of this new-found confidence.

16 Kicked into Touch

'Only rarely do divorced couples stay friends, but something miraculous happened between George and me in the weeks and months after we split up: we did indeed become very good friends. We still loved each other and I never wanted Calum to be estranged from his father, so it would have made no sense for us to be at each other's throats all the time. Despite everything he had put me through, I still wanted what was best for George, for me and for Calum.'

I HAD CALLED CHER and filled her in on everything that had happened, and she immediately offered me a place to live. It was a very tempting offer, but I was determined to make it on my own this time. I wanted to be able to look back and tell people that I had looked after my son and myself without the help of anyone else. Millions of other women had to do it every year, and I knew that if they could, so could I. So despite Cher's kind offer, I decided to stay in San Jose. I rented a little house not far from the family home that had been repossessed. It was nothing fancy, but it was perfect for the two of us.

Only rarely do divorced couples stay friends, but something miraculous happened between George and me in the weeks and months after we split up: we did indeed become very good friends. We still loved each other and I never wanted Calum to be estranged from his father, so it would have made no sense for us to be at each other's throats all the time. Despite everything he had put me through, I still wanted what was best for George, for me and for Calum. George understood that and he knew he had been a terrible husband and father. Almost as soon as we were separated he began to make an effort to behave properly and respectfully around us.

But George always was useless when it came to money, and this trend continued with the child support payments, the first of which was due in July 1982. I hardly ever saw any money because the American lawyers didn't know how to go about getting it from him in London (and he didn't really have that sort of money anyway). I certainly didn't love him and marry him for his money, did I?

I kept in regular contact with George, speaking to him on the phone. He would tell me what he had been doing that week and I would fill him in on Calum's progress. Then one day in August I called him and I could tell he was on edge. I knew he was trying to tell me something but was too nervous to just say it. He finally blurted out that he was dating Mary Stavin. He must have been expecting me to be upset, but I just wished him all the happiness in the world. I truly hoped he could find some peace.

The next month I paid a visit to England for my mother's birthday. While I was there I decided to stay until at least Christmas so that Calum and George could spend some decent time together, and I let George see his son any time he wanted to. I made moves to sort a flat out in London, with a view also to eventually giving up my little house in San Jose. As soon as I arrived I started to make arrangements for some nanny care for Calum every now and then so that I could have a bit of breathing space and go out to restaurants and clubs. I suppose in a way I was trying to show George and everyone else that I was doing just fine, thank you, in charge of and enjoying my life to the full, but I was also trying to fill a void in much the same way I had when I became a Bunny Girl. During the day and when Calum was awake, I devoted myself to him and never had time to dwell on anything else, but evenings were lonely. Don't get me wrong: I wasn't by any stretch of the imagination looking for another man to replace George, I just wanted to be around friends, having some fun. So, in the knowledge that my son was in the hands of a very capable carer – or, occasionally, with his grandparents – I partied in Tramp and Stringfellows.

Then in October George called to tell me that he was moving in with Mary Stavin. I wasn't particularly happy with this news because Mary had never appeared to be receptive where Calum was concerned. It seemed to me that she only just about tolerated him, and I had never seen her cuddle him, hold his hand or even speak to him for that matter. Most of the time I think she just ignored him. Of course I had no problem with George moving in with any woman so long as it made him happy, but I was concerned about the arrangement for Calum's sake. Consequently, I went out of my way to be nice to her as I knew she would be looking after my son at least some of the time. But that didn't really work, and I know that in the end George noticed that Calum was little more than an annoyance to Mary too, and it turned him off her as well. Mary wanted to be famous, and that entailed posing for photographers (with Calum, if necessary) and getting her picture in the paper as often as she could.

Throughout all this I was still seeing George as his friend and the mother of his child. It's very difficult not to spend time together when you have a young child, and anyway, I think it's important for a child to see his or her parents together and getting along, even if they are separated. No matter how bad the break-up has been, parents should always put their children first. Luckily, George and I agreed on this point, so we still managed to have some great days with Calum. But even though I was putting across the image of a single mother coping perfectly well on her own, at this stage in my life I think I was as lost as George was, so that was another reason, albeit unspoken, why each of us needed the other as a friend.

Life persisted in being tough. At this time in London all the papers were running stories saying that Mary Stavin had broken up our marriage and that George had dumped me for her, but that could not have been further from the truth. As much as I disliked Mary, she never had anything to do with the marriage break-up and I could never blame her in any way for what happened. The truth is that I served George with the divorce papers at the end of April and he met Mary a few months after that. And to her credit, when the papers asked Mary about it she also told them she was not responsible for the break-up of our marriage. That should have been the end of the story, but the papers carried on printing it anyway, which was very unfair to all three of us. The press continued to hound me every day. Admittedly I never really minded having my photo in the paper after a night out, but not when the accompanying story told untruths about my life. Sometimes the press can be really horrible. So long as the Angie/George/Mary triangle tales sold their rags, they were happy.

I was becoming restless again, and not just because of harsh treatment from the press. I hardly knew anyone in London. I thought that if I went out every night I would meet people and make friends, but the people I was meeting were just acquaintances really. Being away from England for so long had left me completely out of touch with everything that was happening, and soon all my good intentions of making it on my own in the capital city started to dissolve. I was in two minds: did I want to stay and tough it out in London, or move back to San Jose? My family and Calum's dad were in London, but my real friends, like Cher and Josephine, were in California. I decided to give England a few more weeks and threw myself into an even more hectic schedule of socialising in an effort to make myself feel more secure with the people and the place, but in truth it never even began to work for me. Then Lindy called to tell me that my house in San Jose had been burgled and that some of my possessions had been stolen. 'You've got to decide, Angie,' she begged me. 'Make a decision about where you want to be.' But for reasons I've already explained, I just didn't feel I could.

While I was trying to sort my head out over this issue, Mary Stavin caused another problem for me. I had tried to be courteous to her but it was becoming more and more difficult, mainly because I felt she wasn't very gracious. My sister and I went to Tramp one night and she walked up to me at the table and said patronisingly, 'Oh, you're brave.' I think she wanted to get a reaction out of me because she was in there with George and there were lots of photographers waiting outside, but I couldn't have cared less. Mary then added, 'How could you do this? How could you be here?' I just turned to her and replied, 'Mary, it's OK, everything is fine. I don't mind. George can do what he likes.' Of course this just offended her all the more because I think she expected me to be clingy and still in need of George's presence in my life; she must have thought I was just pretending not to care.

I believe Mary was also jealous of me because George was still drinking at this time, and after a binge he would turn up on my doorstep instead of going home to her. There were times when it felt as if we were still married. I usually let him in, because on the few occasions when I refused he would either manage to barge his way in or make so much noise that he would wake up Calum or the neighbours. It was just easier to let him in, listen to him for half an hour and then send him on his way. Occasionally he would pass out on the couch, but mostly I tried to shield his drunkenness from Calum, although he would be so excited if he woke up in the morning to find his dad lying on the sofa.

Come December George was drinking more and more and the calls were getting more and more frequent. He called me one night and asked me to meet him in a pub. He sounded so desolate and lonely that I agreed to meet him, but by the time I got there Mary Stavin was already sitting next to him and the sight of me just made her blood boil. George had obviously got himself into a mood with her earlier in the evening and had called me wanting to talk. 'What are you doing here?' she spluttered. That little episode pretty much describes our relationship. We didn't like each other but tolerated each other for George's sake. I knew that I irritated the hell out of her but I had no intention of going out of my way to avoid her.

About a week before Christmas I was invited down to the set of the Bond film *Octopussy* by a very good friend of mine who was a Bond girl in the movie. Mary Stavin had a role in the movie as well. So there I was swanning around the set, probably to Mary's displeasure, and I decided to take the opportunity to speak to her and offer some advice about George who, I knew from newspaper articles and his visits to my flat, was at that time behaving like his old self. In other words, he was falling out of nightclubs in full view of photographers and going missing for days on end. So I pulled her to one side to talk to her as I had been through it all and no matter how much I disliked her I didn't want anyone else to put up with what I had gone through. But she said she didn't need my advice, and reacted very negatively. But I had approached her in good faith; why should I want to antagonise the woman who spent quite a bit of time with my son? Calum was always my main interest in all my dealings with Mary. I didn't care what happened to me or what she said about me, it was all about Calum's welfare as far as I was concerned.

George made up for any unfriendliness I felt Mary showed towards me. It was nearly Christmas, and for the first time since we had split I was beginning to feel depressed at the thought of spending the holidays on my own. Set against that, His Lordship and I were getting on as well as ever, and even though George was often dazed, confused and drunk, he always tried to do the right thing. He would give me money every now and then, would try to take care of me and try to be a good dad. He was being really sweet. He would even escort me to Tramp on occasion, although I tried to stop going there with him because he would still get jealous if another man paid me any attention, and there was also Mary to consider, of course. One night I danced with Roger Moore. It was nothing more than friendly fun, but His Lordship saw red. But let's face it, he never saw any other colour when he'd had a few. True to form, at six the next morning he came round to my flat and tried to barge his way in.

I ate my first Christmas lunch without George in six years with my mother and father in Southend. Calum's grandma, and especially his grandpa, fussed over him, and we had a great time. George carried on the fun late that day when he came to my flat bringing with him lots of presents for Calum. I came close to tears as I watched George's eyes light up as he played the proud father, his son gleefully ripping wrapping paper off the gifts. Over the years George has always been there for Calum, albeit often at the end of a phone, but that day was so special to all of us because, despite the split, we felt like a family again, and that's a warm feeling.

But my 1982 was to end on a sour note when I lost a beautiful diamond ring that Allen Schwartz had given me many years before. It was all very over-the-top and glamorous, but I'd had it made into a sensible little ring that I could wear, with just a band of diamonds set around a ruby. I lost it on New Year's Eve in Stringfellows when I went to the bathroom. I took it off so that I didn't snag my tights with it and put it on top of the cistern, then forgot to put it back on. I called the club later, but no one had handed it in. There is someone out there right now wearing a gorgeous, one-of-a-kind diamond ring which belongs to me and to which I have a great sentimental attachment still.

Of course, that experience didn't put me off my love of clubs, and in the early days of 1983 I was back in Tramp. It seems amazing to me now that I used to go there on my own. Normally it was a 'no women without men' type of environment, but I could just swan in on my own, have some champagne and not really be bothered by anyone. It was a very nice feeling to be so privileged, to be able to be so at ease in such an environment. Usually if a woman goes into a club on her own she is harassed by men all night, but His Lordship could usually be found in the club most nights, and while he didn't glue himself to my side, he would keep an eye on me, so most of the guys in Tramp left me alone. It was a good example of the handiness of having carried the name Mrs George Best.

But one night when I was there that January, George was nowhere to be seen. In the early hours of the morning he came staggering in and I was horrified to see that he was covered in blood. Someone had hit him over the head with a pint glass. The blood, which had obviously been gushing out of the gash on his head at one point, had dried by that time and had matted his hair. He looked terrible. He obviously needed stitches, but that was the last thing on his mind. I finally got out of him what had happened, and for once it was not George's fault.

He had been sober and had just been having a quiet night out with Mary when he decided to pop into the bar Chequers in St James's. That turned out to be a big mistake. There were two guys at the bar who for some reason felt they needed to have a go at George, who was minding his own business. His Lordship said that one of the guys just came up behind him and without a word of warning smashed a glass over his head. Mary, seeing the blood pumping out of the wound, ran off to call the police and an ambulance. George, in shock and in pain, instinctively chased after this guy, grabbed him outside and began to bang his head on the pavement. The police soon arrived but didn't charge George with assault after the bar owner confirmed that the attack on him had been completely unprovoked. George was taken to the hospital but after waiting a while to be treated he walked out of the emergency room. Mary wanted him to go home and refused to take him to Tramp, but he was so determined to get back to the comfortable surroundings of a familiar place after his ordeal (and to have a drink) that he hailed a cab and came down to the club on his own.

It may sound cruel, but I couldn't help but laugh as he told me this story. At that time it still wasn't that common for someone to pick on His Lordship – it was usually the other way round when he was drunk. Nevertheless, he of course had a right not to be attacked in the street, and I managed to talk him into going to the police and filing charges against his assailant. The man that had carried out the attack (he was caught by the police at the scene) got off lightly with a three-month suspended sentence, which infuriated George, but there was nothing he could do about it.

Despite all these dramas, which I had left George to get away from, come February I finally made a decision about where I was going to live my life – in favour of the UK. As always, Calum was uppermost in my thoughts, and I felt that the only way he could get the best of both worlds, as it were, was if his mother and father lived in the same country. So I took him off to his grandparents', and on 3 February George took me to the airport and a flight back to San Jose. I wanted to sell everything I had there, finalise things completely and settle down for good in London. But the minute my plane left the tarmac, George went missing, this time for nine days, and everyone began to blame me for sending George on the bender! I just explained that no one but George puts himself in that frame of mind, that we were separated and I wasn't responsible for his actions anyway. The minute I arrived back in London, he resurfaced.

It wasn't long before I was regretting my decision to cut all ties in California. I still had good friends there, and I could still ring them any time, but it felt strange. I felt I'd destroyed part of my life. I kept trying to tell myself I was doing the right thing, but again I felt broke, miserable and lonely in London.

Within a few weeks of returning, I called George and asked him to meet me for a chat as I wanted to talk to him about my feelings, and I knew he would understand. We met for tea at Fortnum and Mason's, and the minute I saw him enter the room, and I don't know why, I burst into tears. There I was in this posh tearoom crying my eyes out, but George just reached out and held me, reminding me fleetingly why I fell in love with him in the first place – which made me cry even more! Of course, as I was sobbing my heart out, Mary Stavin came striding in. But George then did something for which I shall forever be grateful: he stood up and politely but firmly told Mary to leave. It meant a great deal to me at that moment. And to her credit, Mary did not make a scene; she just turned on her heels and walked right out. During the ensuing conversation George talked candidly about his relationship with Mary, that he had finally realised he really didn't have much in common with her and that he also felt she was indifferent towards Calum. We held each other again in that tearoom, and at that point we knew we would be friends for ever, no matter what happened.

George did indeed break it off with Mary later that year, and I went back to the role of his caretaker for a while, making sure he was taking his pills and eating properly. He had just signed for AFC Bournemouth for the 1983/84 season, and for the second time in his life His Lordship seemed utterly determined to get back on track. He even let me check him into Greyshott Hall health farm for some rest and relaxation.

I was perfectly content to look after George at that time. It was like caring for a relative rather than a husband or a lover because there were no complications and rarely any rows. Those months were made easier because throughout the latter half of 1983 and most of 1984 I was living an idyllic life, a life which nonetheless would end in huge complications of my own. For in May 1983 I'd met a man who would take me to hell and back – and all because I had been Mrs George Best.

17 Out of the Frying Pan . . .

'George's imprisonment had a profound effect on Calum. Unfortunately, he'd managed to figure out from the radio that his father had been sent to prison. I hadn't told him about it as I didn't think that at the age of three, nearly four, he needed to know that occasionally his daddy was a silly man.'

CHRISTOPHER CARAJOHN WAS a conman. Plain and simple. He duped a lot of innocent people who lost a lot of money, and eventually he paid the price by going to jail. He also conned me.

It was May 1983 when I first encountered Carajohn. I was at home in London when I received a call from an American man telling me that my good friend Josephine had given him my number (Josephine has a lot to answer for now!). He said that he was new in London, didn't know anybody and would I like to have dinner with him? I was feeling a little down at the time, so I accepted, thinking it might cheer me up. And having dinner with a tall, dark Greek-American did cheer me up a bit, but little did I know that he would be the cause of one of the most depressing episodes in my life.

I didn't fancy Carajohn, he was far too brash and wasn't my type at all. After that dinner I thanked him, but made it perfectly clear I wasn't interested in taking things any further. That did not deter him; in fact, it seemed to make him all the more keen. He called me constantly. Every day the phone would ring and Carajohn would be on the other end. I would end every conversation by telling him that I was perfectly happy as I was and that I didn't need another man in my life, but nothing I said could persuade him to leave me alone. Then he started sending me gifts and flowers. Every day something would arrive at the flat. A dozen red roses here, a little trinket there; in fact, my flat had more flowers in it than furniture for the whole month. I tried to send the gifts back but he wouldn't accept them, and his attitude was starting to worry me. His generosity seemed to be never-ending, for little reason. Any woman loves to receive gifts, but not necessarily from someone for whom you feel nothing, romantically speaking.

One day in the middle of June I agreed to have lunch with Carajohn, and I went with every intention of telling him once and for all to stop behaving in this way. He, of course, was elated because he thought he'd finally won me over. We were sitting in a restaurant in London and I was feeling very awkward when he suddenly blurted out, 'You shouldn't be living in a flat, you should be living in a house in the country. A woman of your calibre should be living in a country manor.' He poured kind words all over me, and by the end of the lunch his charm had begun to work. He actually offered me a house in the country with no strings attached, and was incredibly persuasive. I have to say that it seemed a much better proposition than being a hard-up lost soul in London. All of a sudden, this Carajohn character with whom I'd got more and more irritated over the last few weeks started to intrigue me.

He invited me there and then to go with him to look at some houses, and his assistant picked us up in a stretch limousine and drove us out to Maidenhead and Marlow where Carajohn had arranged for an estate agent to show us around. I knew in my soul that I shouldn't really accept any of this amazing generosity because I still had absolutely no intention of giving him anything in return. It never once occurred to me then that Carajohn might be using me, I just wouldn't have believed it of him. Again, my naivety, mixed this time with a bit of greed (but then conmen play on people's hopes, fears and weaknesses, don't they?), reared its silly little head, and I began to be seduced by Carajohn's talk about all the things he wanted to do for me because he liked me so much.

I viewed an amazing old parsonage in Marlow that afternoon, and by the end of the first week in July Carajohn had arranged it so that I could move in with

Calum, his nanny and a housekeeper. I felt like the madam of the manor. The parsonage was owned by the musician Jim Capaldi from the band Traffic, and Carajohn told me he'd rented it through an agent. Without realising it, I was about to fall hook, line and sinker into a trap. Carajohn had demanded absolutely nothing in return, other than my company at dinner every now and then. He would take care of me, he said. Yes, it was a little too good to be true, but it seemed real at the time. The papers reported that I'd moved in with Carajohn, but he stayed in his flat while Calum and I lived in the parsonage, which was the perfect arrangement for me because I wasn't ready for any kind of commitment and Carajohn knew that. I just put it down to him being a wealthy, generous American. Of course now I know that he was using me as a sort of promotional gimmick. His aim was to be seen in town with me, to get his picture in the papers so he could play up his prestige and meet new clients whom he could rip off.

During this time George was happily ensconced in a little house in Chelsea. I spoke to him occasionally on the phone, but didn't have a great deal of contact with him because I had left the London party scene behind. Instead, I was living a new, surreal life. Carajohn kept on plying me with presents day in, day out. Limousines would arrive at the house with presents on board. He sometimes asked me to meet him for tea at the Ritz. On one occasion as I sipped from my cup, Carajohn handed over a box which contained a beautiful pair of diamond earrings; on another it was a fur coat. One week he gave me a fabulous bronze; the following week the limousine picked me up and whisked me off to Bond Street to go shopping (Carajohn had even opened up charge accounts in various department stores for me). Once after a shopping trip I arranged the clothes I had bought in my wardrobe, looked at them and thought, 'What next?' Well, next up was a full set of Louis Vuitton luggage. It was never-ending. It just went on and on and on, and I, like a greedy, unthinking girl, didn't say no to any of it.

At one stage my mother, a little worried herself, called him and suggested the gifts were a little too much, but I never once thought to question any of it, as I had done when I first met Carajohn, a fact which I deeply regret now. As Josephine said, 'There is no such thing as a free lunch.' Maybe if I had stepped back and taken a moment to think about it, I would have realised that something was wrong, but at the time I thought all these material possessions would make me happy. How wrong I was.

Then the cars started coming, and before long Carajohn would send me off to various balls, film premières and functions all dressed up. He would go to some of them with me, say his name and literally introduce himself to everybody there. Then, at the end of July, along came my thirty-first birthday and Carajohn, along with his colleague Michael Lewis – who was later given the dubious title 'walker', which is someone who escorts a lady to a function – decided he was going to throw what he called an 'emerald ball' for me. The main reason it was called that was my present: an antique Cartier necklace with eight rows of draped pearls and an emerald centrepiece. It was the most magnificent gift anyone had ever given me.

The £15,000 party was held at Brocket Hall, a stately home in Hertfordshire, and more than 300 celebrities turned up to wish me a happy birthday (I knew about three of them). The guests were greeted by emerald-coloured footmen who offered them glasses of Krug champagne, and were entertained by midgets, conjurors, fire-eaters, a human scarecrow and a robot. Carajohn had also arranged for a huge firework display to be held at midnight, but as the fireworks shot into the air, neighbours living in the nearby estate called the police to complain about the noise and officers arrived and tried to shut the party down. Carajohn agreed to stop the fireworks, but the champagne kept flowing all night. The party was a success; we even made it on to the front cover of the *Mail on Sunday* magazine, which was Carajohn's aim all along. (I believe he knew when he gave me the necklace what was happening in his business and that the necklace, along with everything else, would never even get warm on my neck.)

Yes, the entire party was staged as a grand photo opportunity for Carajohn, with me, his dupe, at his side. Nigel Dempster from the *Mail* was there, and so was the *Express*'s Richard Young. It was just another way for Carajohn to show potential clients that he was well known and had the right connections. Carajohn never discussed with me what he did for a living, and I never asked. I knew he was some sort of investment banker, but beyond that I didn't have a clue. It was the same when I was with His Lordship: I knew George kicked a ball around a pitch for a living, but I couldn't have held a conversation with him on the finer points of the game. I just wasn't that interested. Of course I was informed later by the police about the true nature of Christopher Carajohn, and that he was known for pulling the same kind of stunts in New York.

As for His Lordship, he made it clear he was happy for me and couldn't have cared less about Carajohn; he was still madly in love with Mary Stavin at the time. Once, after they had had a blazing row and she had thrown him out, George even came to the parsonage to stay for a while with Calum and me. There seemed to him to be nothing fishy about the arrangement either. Carajohn, of course, was perfectly happy for George to stay with us – just more publicity for him.

So I was very content with my new life and my beautiful house and my Mercedes with heated seats (heaven in the winter), and not once during all that time – over a year – did I even so much as suspect that Carajohn was using me. And when I did figure out that the arrangement wasn't all it seemed to be, it was more of a gradual realisation than a blinding flash of knowledge. I think I must have come across a newspaper article one day which spoke of Christopher Carajohn's business dealings, about him only being famous by association with me, and that that was how he got all his 'clients'. That was the key phrase: famous by association with me, just as I was famous by association with George. It was all very weird.

Everything came crashing down for both of us in September 1984 when Carajohn was arrested on a charge of stealing millions of pounds from his clients. It was the Cinderella story in reverse for me: I had a very happy and comfortable lifestyle, I went to the ball and when the clock struck at the end of the day I left with nothing, with no glass slipper to resurrect my fortunes. When Carajohn got caught, virtually everything went with him: the Mercedes, the designer clothes, the outlandish gifts and, of course, the jewellery. It was a shock when it happened, but to tell you the truth I couldn't give all this expensive stuff back quick enough. The newspapers had reported the value of the jewellery alone at something like half a million pounds, which I now knew was other people's money, their life savings. One poor man, it was reported, even killed himself because his savings had been taken by Carajohn. I felt awful that all these people had been swindled and that I had unknowingly reaped the benefits. Carajohn's lawyers had demanded that I hand back all the expensive items, but I thought it an insult even to think that I needed telling.

That man had given me more materially in just over a year than I had ever had in thirty, but all he left me with was a very sour taste in my mouth. I was well shot of him. In fact, I had begun to feel miserable even before I found out the truth, because I'd begun for the first time to allow myself to realise that Carajohn wasn't throwing gifts at me out of love and affection, but instead with some sort of selfish motive (even though I hadn't yet figured out what sort of motive). What was missing for me was love. I was never in any doubt that I could have pretty much anything I wanted – I had a house full of material possessions, for goodness' sake – but it meant nothing without love and affection to go with it. I fooled myself for many months into thinking that I could substitute happiness with diamonds and furs and allowed myself to be seduced by the smell of money. I should have known better than that.

At the conclusion of the trial in 1985, Carajohn was sent down for seven years with his partner Graeme Allison (who had actually brought Carajohn in to lend the scam some business credibility) after the jury found them guilty of using a £100 off-the-shelf company to fleece investors of 'mind-boggling' sums of money. This 'investment company' had been set up and wealthy clients courted and cheated of millions by the pair claiming that the money was being invested on the American stock market. The prosecution called Carajohn 'a fast, persuasive talker' and 'the leading villain in the enterprise'. I was one of his victims, even though I didn't actually lose a penny of my own.

By that time I had already taken steps to cut Carajohn entirely out of my life, but of course during those last few months of 1984 the press had a field day with the story, especially when in December George was jailed as well, for drink-driving and assaulting a policeman. One Friday night His Lordship decided to take his car out when he knew he was going to be drinking. He was usually very responsible about things like that, but on this particular night he got behind the wheel of his Jag, which was a big mistake. The police pulled him over near Buckingham Palace, breathalysed him and took him to the nearest station. They processed him and released him. His Lordship, for a change, didn't go off to have a drink but went straight home to bed.

The following afternoon he ambled down to the pub, and got the shock of his life when his drinking buddies told him there was a warrant out for his arrest because he had failed to turn up at court that morning. George said the police had never told him that he had to go to court and had assumed he would be told in due course when he had to put in an appearance. But instead of going straight down to the local nick to hand himself in, he decided to have a drink instead.

He eventually made it home in the early hours of Sunday morning and thought nothing more about the incident until someone rang his doorbell a few hours later. Thinking it was a tabloid reporter, His Lordship yelled 'Piss off!', but he soon found out that it was a police officer on the other side of the door. Still George had no intention of giving himself up, and he went back to bed, despite what was actually quite a heavy police presence in the street. After a brief nap he decided to make a run for it to the house of a girl he knew across the road, and after checking that the coast was clear he sprinted across. As he did so, several policemen appeared and tried to grab him. George finally surrendered, but not until he'd put up a bit of a struggle during which he headbutted one of the policemen. They shoved him into the back of a van and took him to the station where they held him until it was time for him to face the judge on Monday morning. With charges hanging over him that included drink-driving, failing to appear in court and assaulting a police officer, George was sent down for three months, spending eight days in Pentonville before being transferred to the lower-security Ford open prison – where, coincidentally, Christopher Carajohn was being held.

Well, the papers loved it. They all printed huge articles on how both my men were in prison together, Carajohn for embezzlement and George for being George. Everyone seemed to think it was one big joke, but I was so ashamed. They weren't even 'my men' at the time. I'd had absolutely no intention of visiting Carajohn, and I didn't go and see George either. I gave them both (particularly Carajohn) a wide berth.

Not that George needed me to go and see him. At the time he was with a wonderful young woman called Angie Lynn. She was an absolute doll, one of the nicest women George has ever dated. I got on really well with her too. She understood that George still had ties to me because of Calum, and she went out of her way to be friendly and accommodating. Angie was the one visiting His Lordship in prison, she was the one taking care of George. I was too busy making sure Calum was all right.

George's imprisonment had a profound effect on Calum. Unfortunately, he'd managed to figure out from the radio that his father had been sent to prison. I hadn't told him about it as I didn't think that at the age of three, nearly four, he needed to know that occasionally his daddy was a silly man. After he'd got wind of what had happened, I struggled to explain things to him, to tell him why his father wouldn't be coming with presents and dressing up as Santa (as he'd done the year before) on Christmas Day. Calum, of course, hadn't fully understood the news report on the radio, and after hearing my version of events he simply turned to me and blubbed, 'I don't want my daddy to be in prison.' It broke my heart to see him so upset. All I could say in reply was, 'Well, Daddy will be staying there for a while but he will come and see you very soon.'

I would never have badmouthed George in front of Calum; moreover, despite this latest brush with the law, I had no reason to. George had been very supportive when the Christopher Carajohn fiasco unfolded around me in September, which was especially heartwarming because I hadn't spoken to George that much while I was living in the lap of luxury at the parsonage – another aspect of that whole episode that I was sorry for. But part of the reason for not contacting His Lordship that much was because he seemed to be getting on with his life very well. George was never exactly one for being a model citizen, but over the last year or so he'd done himself proud.

It had been a crazy year, and once again I found myself on the threshold of a new one hoping for brighter prospects. And I wasn't altogether to be disappointed.

18 The Emerging Woman

'Val Kilmer was charming company, and even then had a big-star air about him. He would walk into a room as if he had every right to be there, almost as if he owned the place, but managed to do it gracefully. His Lordship could charm the birds out of the trees, but he never possessed that kind of attitude. Whenever he went somewhere he would just walk through the door and head straight for the bar or the back of the room. People would, of course, flock to him because he was George Best, but Val commanded people's attention even before fame arrived.'

IT MIGHT SOUND as though my life has been one miserable moment after another, but that's not the case at all. I know there have been times when had I not laughed I would have cried, but I've had more than my fair share of genuinely light and happy times, even in the midst of problems.

One silly little thing that happened during the Christopher Carajohn saga always makes me smile when I think about it. It was October 1983, and a friend of mine, Lindy Benson, was going out to dinner with Omar Sharif, whom she was dating at the time. She invited me and my mother to accompany them. We went to Langan's, where my mother proceeded to have a blazing row with Omar over his attitude to women. Really Omar is a very nice man, it's just that when it comes to the opposite sex the culture he comes from has different views from Western ones. Some may call them chauvinistic, but then that is how men from the Arab world live their lives. Of course Omar, having spent a great part of his life outside his native Egypt, is more liberal and enlightened than many of his fellow countrymen, but still traditional enough to upset my mother. There was no way she was going to stand for it; she didn't care what religion or culture he was from. Lindy and I were both trying not to laugh as she tore a strip off our movie heart-throb, but he managed to turn his charm on and come the end of the dinner they were the best of friends.

My mum could be so prim and proper sometimes. I remember another occasion, just after the filming of His Lordship's second appearance on *This Is Your Life* in 1983, when a group of us went off to Tramp and got a table so that we could order some food. At that time the club had a very popular dish – nothing fancy, just plain old bangers and mash, but it was the way it was served that made it famous. You see, the sausages and mashed potatoes were arranged on the plate in the shape of a penis and testicles. My mother nearly had a heart attack when she saw it, and refused to eat it. She was yelling at the poor waiters: 'Take it back! I couldn't possibly eat it like that!' Johnny Gold, the owner-manager of Tramp, was as good as his name. He took my mum's plate back to the kitchen, rearranged the food, brought it back and managed to placate my mother.

Also during the Carajohn affair, I was reminded that nights out with men could be just as enjoyable as nights out with the girls or my mother. In Tramp one evening about a month after my mother's 'food problem', I met someone who showed me that there were men out there who always put women first and treated them well. His name was Eddie Kidd, the stunt motorcycle rider who had become famous after appearing in a sexy Levis advert. I met him purely by chance, because at the time, tucked up in my lovely parsonage in Marlow with my lovely son, I wasn't going out much at all in London. The clubs had literally begun to lose their appeal for me; what I really wanted to do was spend my evenings at home with Calum, especially as he was now growing up quickly. Occasionally, though, one of my girlfriends would talk me into going out for the evening, and it was on one of those nights that I met Eddie.

I went out for dinner as part of a big group, and he was there. At first I didn't take much notice of him, but by the end of the evening he had moved round the table to sit next to me. We spent the rest of the night talking – or rather I did. It was just so nice to talk to a man and have him actually listen to me. Eddie just sat there and took in every word I said, every now and then prompting me with a question about myself. I found it such a refreshing experience that when he asked if he could take me out to dinner the following week, I found myself saying yes. We became good friends. I wasn't looking for a relationship, and Eddie was very understanding as he had just split from his wife, a dancer with Hot Gossip. He was exactly what I needed at that stage in my life.

And in May 1984 Cher came to London. We went out dancing as it had been so long since we'd had a girls' night out together. I went to pick her up at the St James Club, a lovely, discreet little hotel where she was staying, and when I went up to her room I found she was with a guy, whom she introduced as Val Kilmer (this was before *Top Gun* had helped to make him into a film star, so I needed the introduction). It turned out that Cher was dating him and they were staying together at the hotel. We had a great time together that night and for the next few days before she and Val flew back to Los Angeles.

Five months later, as I was sitting at home trying to cope with the immediate aftermath of the Carajohn revelations, the phone rang. I was shocked to find Val on the other end of the line. I had absolutely no idea where he'd got my number from, but he wanted to know if I would like to go out to dinner. My first question was 'Where's Cher?' but Val simply said, 'I don't date her any more.' I was flattered by the proposal, and certainly had no objections to having dinner with him, but I put him off for a short while because I wanted to speak to Cher first. So I called her and told her the story. When I asked her if she minded, she said no, but I'm not sure whether or not she meant it because she didn't get in contact with me for a good year after that.

So I called Val and arranged to pick him up at the St James Club, where he was staying. We had a good time and he helped to cheer me up. I dated Val for a while after that. He was charming company, and even then had a big-star air about him. He would walk into a room as if he had every right to be there, almost as if he owned the place, but managed to do it gracefully. His Lordship could charm the birds out of the trees, but he never possessed that kind of attitude. Whenever he went somewhere he would just walk through the door and head straight for the bar or the back of the room. People would, of course, flock to him because he was George Best, but Val commanded people's attention even before fame arrived. Again, that romance fizzled out before it became serious, but I had a good, relaxing time with Val and was happy with that. After the Carajohn débâcle, he helped restore my faith in the opposite sex.

When things settled down a bit after those disastrous final months of 1984, I came into a generally happy period in my life. I had moved into a little house in Fifield, near Maidenhead, with Calum and Martin, Calum's male nanny. It was perfect because Martin was always there to help and was fantastic with Calum. He had originally been my handyman and had fixed the place up for me, but then I asked him to stay on and look after Calum because he could do all the boy things with him that a female nanny probably couldn't do. For instance, he took Calum and his friends camping, stayed overnight in treehouses and played football. All of us were having a wonderful time.

As those early months of 1985 wore on I began to feel that my life was well and truly back on track. In fact, my self-confidence had probably never been higher. Early that year I decided to start a PR company with my girlfriend Charlie Spry, and we began to publicise things like restaurant openings and film premières. We helped promote, for instance, the first showings of *Platoon*, starring Charlie Sheen and Tom Berenger. Also at this time Warner Brothers announced their intention to make a movie of George's life. I owned the rights to His Lordship's autobiography *Where Do I Go from Here?* (George had signed them over to me so that I could sell them when the time seemed right, for Calum's benefit), so executives from Warner Brothers approached me with their idea. We soon struck a deal as a result of which they bought those rights, but the film was never made. The British papers accused me of being too secretive about the sums involved, but at the time I couldn't talk money because we hadn't yet reached or signed the final agreement. And shortly after that the BBC approached me. They wanted to film a pilot for a health and fitness programme and wanted me to front it. I was so excited that they'd asked me to do this, and I spent weeks in a studio putting together a show which I thought was very good. Unfortunately, the BBC shelved the idea before it hit the screens, and that was the end of my very brief TV career. Still, it was all good experience and added to my ever-growing confidence.

And to add to all of that, I had woken up one morning with a fabulous idea to take the dieting programme I followed, which was a mix of food combining and exercise, and teach it to whoever would listen. So I immediately called Penny, my secretary, and said, 'We have to do a road show and we have to get a sponsor.' So we approached some companies potentially willing to back us, managed to get Reebok and Univite - a health drink supplement company at whose premises I had once given a talk about food combining - on board, and set about organising a twelve-city tour. The food combining philosophy had been introduced to me by Barry Manilow, and I wanted to spread the word to all the girls who needed it. So at each stop I did a lecture, hosted an exercise class and finished with a question-and-answer session. I had a great time, but I suppose our meetings could have been better attended. Given the explosion in popularity of health and fitness in the last decade or so, I think perhaps we were a little ahead of the times. Mind you, I did lead a thousand keep-fit fans into action at a football ground, which proved to be the world's largest aerobic workout and raised funds for the British Olympic appeal.

But before the tour actually started, Penny and I got ourselves into a spot of bother. When we received confirmation that Reebok were happy to back the road show, I decided to take Penny out to dinner to celebrate, so off we went to a local restaurant. When we explained to the owners of the restaurant why we were there, they decided that the celebration should start with a bottle of champagne and end with a glass of brandy each. I was on such a high that I'm sorry to say I didn't for one moment consider the fact that I would be driving home afterwards, and as I'd been on a health drive for quite some time, I soon became a little tipsy (Penny handled the alcohol a lot better).

When we finished our meal, I decided it was time to go, but as we left the restaurant the maître d' advised us to stay and get a taxi, especially as he'd seen a police car sitting in a car park across the street. Again, I'm sorry to say that as soon as I saw the police car I made a snap decision to leave as quickly as possible. Now, I had learned to drive in America and had passed my test in an automatic, the car of choice in the United States. But I had just bought a lovely new manual Porsche Targa, so a quick getaway was probably always out of the question. I gingerly clutched and gear-shifted my way out of the restaurant car park, and carried on down the road until Penny and I were way out of sight of the police car and feeling safe. Then I put on a bit more speed. Now the roads in rural Maidenhead tend to have a lot of very tight S-bends, and you have to be even more careful when driving a Porsche Targa because the engine is in the back of the car which makes it bottom heavy. That night, I wasn't careful, and as I took one of the bends a little faster than I should have done, I lost control of the back end of the car, it spun out of control and hit a brick wall.

No great harm was done – the car was technically a write-off, but we were fine and it turned out that the people whose wall we had hit were used to this kind of thing happening on that bend – and after the initial shock Penny and I looked at each other and burst into hysterical laughter. We just couldn't help ourselves. But the people in the house whose wall we had hit had called the police immediately, and when we heard the sirens we thought we had better hide, so we scrambled out of the car and hid behind a bush. We crouched there for a while, giggling uncontrollably like two teenagers, until eventually a torch shone on to us and a voice said, 'Were you two ladies driving this car?' Penny, still sniggering, said straight away, pointing at me, 'No, she was.' Well, the upshot was that I had to go to court and I was asked to surrender my driving licence for a year. I took my punishment on the chin. The worst part was that it turned out I was only insured for driving an automatic, so all I got for my Porsche was its scrap value, although the reaction of the newspapers the next day was just as bad. They were full of Mrs Best's drink-driving escapades and talk of the two toy-boys I was supposed to have had in the back of my car. Penny and I don't know to this day how on earth that toy-boy angle was ever dragged into it.

Soon after I ended my brief romance with Val Kilmer in the spring of 1985, Christopher Carajohn began contacting me from prison, where he was being held awaiting trial. He would send unpleasant letters still asking me to send everything back. I had already surrendered the great majority of the possessions – which were, after all, effectively stolen goods – as soon as he was sentenced, but now he was demanding that literally *everything* be sent to his lawyers. For instance, Carajohn had given my mother and father a TV and video as a Christmas present, and he wanted that back too. I refused, because my parents had accepted the gift in good faith and there came a point where Carajohn had to accept responsibility for his own actions, but when a few years later he got out of prison (he served less than half his time) he went down to their house and took it back anyway, conveniently forgetting that my trusting parents had actually lent him some money when he needed it. His actions were those, I believe, of a mentally unstable man, and I was afraid of him.

In fact, the whole thing made me physically sick. I had always been very fit and healthy, even when I was spending most of my time trying to deal with His Lordship's dramas, but the stress that Carajohn began to put me through now made me feel under the weather a lot of the time. I was so low that I managed to contract a chest infection during this time, and then pneumonia. It really took its toll on me. Carajohn would even call my mother whenever he got the opportunity, and we both felt terribly threatened by this behaviour. I tried to ignore it, look on the bright side and concentrate on my work (I was working on the BBC pilot show when the problem was at its height).

Then, right in the middle of this absolute hell, I met a rugby player called David Cook. We immediately hit it off, and then off I went on a whirlwind romance with him. He was the most gorgeous, big, blonde sportsman, but as usual it only lasted a couple of months. I wasn't looking for a deep and meaningful relationship that would last the rest of my life anyway; I just felt a real desire for some fun at that stage of my life, and David delivered!

Carajohn carried on hounding me after he was released on bail, pending trial. He kept telling me how much he loved me, how much he wanted to rent another house for me and go back to the way things were – as if I'd fall for that one again! He called me day and night, but this time I knew I was strong enough to resist him. I was the one in charge of the situation, and he didn't like that at all. With this newfound confidence, and because he was being such a pest and I wanted him out of my life completely, I agreed to meet him in July a few days before my thirty-third birthday in order, as far as I was concerned, to tell him exactly where he could go.

I arrived at the restaurant on time, and surprisingly didn't feel nervous about seeing him face to face. We sat down at a table, and before he had even spoken he was up to his old tricks again: he put a box down in front of me. I had no intention of opening it, let alone accepting it, but he reached across, opened the box and held up a glittering diamond necklace for me to see. I felt nothing. A few years earlier I probably would have gasped, but not now. I had matured a lot since then; I was no longer the child in the sweet shop. So I stood up and walked away without looking back.

Of course, that didn't deter him. Some weeks later he

tried to give me a Rolex watch and some pearl earrings. He even went so far as to ask me to marry him. I told him for the umpteenth time to leave me alone, that there was no way on earth any number of diamond necklaces or expensive watches would make me marry him. For the first time in a long time I was depending on me, and me alone, and it felt good. I felt, as they say on the other side of the Atlantic, empowered, and I truly believed that the time had long gone when Christopher Carajohn could affect my life.

George was also doing the right thing with his life during this period, which added to my happiness. On Guy Fawkes Day 1985, I held a huge fireworks party and the whole neighbourhood came. George also turned up, with Angie Lynn. We had dozens and dozens of fireworks, and Calum was so excited that his dad was there. The party was a raging success; it was one of those moments where we were like a family again, celebrating a special occasion together, and I include Angie in that because by that stage she was like one of the family and we got on very well.

My life became manic once more, but in a good way this time. It was an enormous growth period for me, emotionally and business-wise, and I came out the other end a better, wiser, more stable and happy person. When I look back, I am glad that all these things happened to me, traumatic though some of them were, because they made me the person I am today. My only regret is that I wasn't a little more sensible when it came to putting a few things away for a rainy day, but then I always did try to have a good time in life – because it was important to me. It hadn't always been that way, of course. I was always the healthy, sensible one when I was in California with George and Cher, the type who would stay at home. When I was married to His Lordship, I thought that was what wives were supposed to do: stay at home and look after their husbands. Even before we got married, when George went out sometimes I would go with him but more often than not we would just have dinner together and then I would go home. And with Carajohn I would go to the functions he selected and act the way I was asked to act, not the way I wanted to act. But the mid-1980s was my flowering as an independent woman. I made my own decisions in life, I did things my way, the way I wanted to do them, and I had a fantastic time with some fantastic people.

Cher flew into town in the new year, and it was just like the old days with the two of us spending our days shopping and working out and our evenings partying with the best of them. I couldn't live that sort of life now, and I'm so glad I did it when I had the chance. Cher and I got on really well in those early months of 1986, and in March she called me and asked me again to fly to New York to help her work out ahead of the Academy Awards. To be honest I didn't really have to do that much – Cher always kept herself in such fantastic shape – but there was no way I was going to turn down an invitation like that, so I arranged for Calum to stay with his grandparents, flew over and we exercised and food-combined together for three weeks. At the Oscars ceremony that year Cher won in the best actress category for her role in *Moonstruck* and wowed the audience in *that* Bob Mackie dress (which was barely there, to tell the truth). She looked fabulous and I was so proud of her.

While we were in New York, Carajohn called me again. I had no idea how he'd got hold of my number there, but it really was the last straw, and I decided there and then that I had had enough of Christopher Carajohn and my life in London. Apart from his nuisance calls, everything was working out fine, but once again I felt this overpowering need to be back near the palm trees, in the place I had always felt was truly home.

I returned to London and almost immediately began planning to move my life back to California, pushed on by a powerful feeling that no matter what else happened, I would once again feel complete back there. But before I did there were some important matters to attend to, not the least of which was obtaining a decree absolute in my divorce from George (pretty much a formality) and a potential battle for custody of Calum.

19 Just the Two of Us

'After a few hours we left to go to the immigration office, and there my plan worked. Everyone in the office was so delighted at meeting George Best and having autographs signed that they practically issued us with new passports on the spot. Seeing His Lordship standing there in his element, smiling and chatting to those people, made me realise that things would never change for him. I knew then that no matter how old or drunk he got, people would always want to shake his hand so they could tell their friends that they had met the one and only George Best.'

Although no one could say George hadn't taken an interest in his son, he was certainly not what you might call a 'hands-on' dad, so I had no qualms in going to court to ask for sole custody of Calum. As it turned out, it was a formality. On the morning of the hearing in July 1986 I was extremely nervous. I made sure to dress smartly and arrived at the court in plenty of time. The lawyers had told His Lordship all about it, of course, and we all expected him to turn up and at least ask for visitation rights, if not joint custody, but when they called out our names in the courtroom I looked around to see that there was no sign of George. He failed to show up for his own son's custody hearing; I felt this was His Lordship's way of telling me that he knew in his heart of hearts I was the better person to look after Calum. So did the judge, funnily enough.

After that morning in court I had no misgivings about preparing to pack up our things and make the final move, although I was determined not to rush anything. I had discussed it with George when I got back from New York, but I don't think it had really sunk in that I was moving back to Los Angeles and taking Calum with me, even though I'd also gone through all the right legal processes and given George every chance to respond. He was in a very strange emotional place around that time, fuelled by the drink again, of course. I'm not sure he had seen (nor would he see over the coming years) many sober days for months. I desperately wanted Calum, now of school age, not to have to grow up and live his young life watching his drunken father on television, reading about his escapades in the papers and hearing about every last scrape he got into on the radio – and probably getting picked on in the playground because of it. As for Calum, well, I didn't explain the situation fully to him before we left, although he knew that the reason he had been spending quite a bit of time at his grandparents' house was because Mummy was selling everything and getting ready to move back with him to Los Angeles. Calum was born in California but we'd left when he was just a year old, so he wouldn't have had many memories of that time, if any, so there was little point in talking about it from that angle too.

In spite of His Lordship's obvious shortcomings, some people might think it was cruel and selfish of me to move back to America and take George's son away from him, but let me just say this: it actually worked out much better that way. Calum always got to spend every summer holiday – six full weeks – with his dad, which in terms of number of days was a lot more in one calendar year than George had ever spent with his son while we were living in London. The new arrangement focused George's mind a bit more on the responsibilities of fatherhood, and this benefited Calum.

Calum was always my first consideration. Part of the reason why I wanted to move at this time was because, as I said, he had already started to go to school, and I didn't want to have to wrench him out of what would probably be a comfortable routine in a year or so's time. I knew that if I wanted to make the move, I had to take the plunge sooner rather than later. As I made preparations for leaving, Calum attended a private school. His grandpa would take such pride in making sure he looked smart in his school uniform every day: shiny shoes, spotless shirt and a clean cap. Whenever the school did anything that involved the parents I always told George, although never in a million years imagining he would turn up. But once, on the school's annual sports day, he did. Not only did he throw his son completely by putting in an appearance, he also ran in the fathers' race, which he won. Calum could not have been more proud of his dad that day.

I was a little sad to leave England and my parents behind early in January 1987, but I knew Los Angeles was where I wanted to be and I soon fell into a familiar routine over there. Calum and I initially stayed with my sister Lindy for a few weeks in San Jose, but I had a home and a job with Cher waiting for me in Beverly Hills. As it turned out we were in Beverly Hills for a month, but then we moved once again, this time to Malibu. And there was a reason for that choice.

While I was staying with Lindy, I met Terry Arnaud. Lindy and I were at the hairdresser's one day and had just come out when a magnificent blue and white 57 Stingray convertible drove past. In the front seat was this absolutely gorgeous man with long, flowing blonde hair and a suntanned body. In no uncertain terms, I instructed my sister to 'follow that car'. I didn't expect her to because she never usually takes orders from anyone, but in the blink of an eye there we were, speeding down the road and giggling like two teenagers. We eventually pulled up next to this gorgeous creature, and in jest I rolled down the window and shouted to him, 'Are you married?' He said no, so I said, 'Good, pull over.' Much to my surprise, he did! My sister and I just sat there not knowing what to do. What had we got ourselves into? We watched stunned as this handsome hunk got out of his car and walked towards us. All I remember is whispering to my sister, 'Oh my God, he's wearing flip-flops. I've never dated a man who wore flip-flops!'

Terry and I hit it off straight away, and not only did I date him, I married him. Terry was a lovely, kind, sweet man. And he adored Calum. Unfortunately for poor Terry, I wanted to marry him quickly because at that time Cher and I were getting ready to go on the road again, which meant a lot of hard work and dedication. So after we decided to tie the knot I began furiously to make wedding plans, and Cher very kindly said we could use her house overlooking the bluffs in Malibu. I was so excited, and happy. I felt blessed, because literally within weeks of making a life-changing decision, it seemed I'd landed on my feet again.

I called His Lordship and told him that I was getting married again as I thought it only fair that he should know, and he wished me all the best. A lot of people may wonder why I would want to invite my ex-husband to my second marriage, but I wanted George there for Calum, not for me. In my mind it was very important that George gave the OK to this union, for Calum's sake. It just so happened that at the time of the wedding His Lordship was due to stop off in Los Angeles after playing an exhibition match in San Jose, and he agreed to attend the ceremony if I sorted out some transport for him. No problem. I arranged for a car to pick George up from Los Angeles airport and bring him to Cher's home in Malibu. Calum was thrilled with the news.

Come the day, Terry and I exchanged vows in front of our close friends, and everything went smoothly. It was only when the ceremony ended that I realised His Lordship hadn't made it. I was not as upset about it as Calum, though. I still had a good time without George there, but Calum was heartbroken that his dad hadn't been able to make what was a twenty-mile journey from the airport to Cher's house. I later found out that George hadn't even bothered to wait for the car I'd sent, but had instead jumped straight into a cab and gone directly to Bestie's – now owned by Bobby McAlinden. His Lordship insisted that the car had never turned up, that he'd decided instead to go and see Bobby for a few hours until his flight back to London, and that he didn't get drunk, but as far as I was concerned he had done one of his usual disappearing acts. At the very least a phone call to let Calum know that he wouldn't be able to make it would have been nice. I was disappointed with George, because lately he had been pretty dependable. He had been sending me money for Calum and had been ringing him every week to spend an hour or so chatting on the phone. So to let him down in that way made me more upset than angry. But, as I said, I refused to let it ruin my big day, and we soon gathered round to cheer Calum up as we carried on the celebrations into the evening.

My second wedding ran in stark contrast to my first. Then it had been a fiasco in a Las Vegas wedding chapel: dodging the press, George getting drunk and looking awful, me looking awful too – it was just a shambles in so many ways. Getting hitched to Terry could not have been more different. Instead of a schoolmarmish suit I wore a gorgeous wedding dress borrowed from the designer Bob Mackie, we had beautiful rings to put on each other's fingers, and the whole thing was magnificent. It felt like a proper wedding.

Terry and I had a good relationship, but I was working with Cher and three weeks away on tour and one week at home does not a marriage make. Sadly, after a couple of years of this, poor Terry decided he'd had enough, and who can blame him? It was a mutual parting of the ways, and we stayed friends.

So it was back to being just Calum and me. For the next few years everything went swimmingly for us. Nobody in America really knew who George Best was, and more importantly no one cared. This helped because I'd planned for Calum to live a relatively carefree and normal life (if you can call living with Cher and having her as an 'aunt' normal, of course!). I was a handful to put up with on occasion, though. In September 1990 we were all in Aspen for the wedding of Cher's sister Georganne. Cher and I had been on the road and had spent the past few months travelling to Sacramento, Oakland, Seattle, Vancouver and Calgary. We had even stopped off in New York. But we made sure we were in Aspen for Georganne's wedding to Ed Bartalak, Cher's bodyguard. We were all staying in a little house in Aspen, and the day before the wedding Cher called me upstairs for some reason, but as I bounded up the stairs I caught my foot at a funny angle and broke it. I was in miserable, agonising pain, and had to go straight to the local hospital to have my whole leg put in a cast. So there I was in the wedding group with a leg in plaster, looking as if I was doing my damnedest to upstage Georganne on her special day.

Apart from that embarrassing incident, I have very fond memories of that trip to Aspen. In fact, that Christmas I took Calum there for the holidays. I had a very dear friend at the time called Susan Hamilton. She had a son Calum's age, and they quickly became good friends. So Susan and I decided to take our boys (we were both single mothers) with another friend of theirs to Aspen for Christmas. We rented a lovely apartment which cost a fortune, so we decided to drive up to Colorado rather than fly to save a bit of money. I had a Toyota 4Runner at the time, so we loaded all the suitcases into the car (you would have thought we were going to Europe for six months with all the luggage there was), then the five of us, and set out for Aspen. We planned our route to take in Zion and Brice Parks, natural habitat parks in the state of Utah. You can drive through these parks for hours on end and not see a soul; in fact, we managed nine hours before we had to stop because of fog. We had three weeks in Aspen, and the boys were thrilled because they got to go skiing every day. Susan was also a brilliant cook, which helped a great deal, and there were plenty of things to do for all ages. I didn't ski myself, spending most of my days in the gym instead, but I would go up into the Aspen mountains to meet everyone for lunch. The day before New Year's Eve Calum tried snowboarding for the first time. We had the best Christmas, and all too soon it was time to go back to Los Angeles.

Cher and I had been on the road for several years, but at the end of 1991 came a chance to do something a bit different: the American network CBS asked Cher to do an exercise video, and it was decided that I would help her do it. Our workouts consisted largely of a routine devised by Cher's choreographer Damita Jo Freeman, which Cher had been doing for the past twelve years. We showed the routine to Steven Poe, an executive at CBS, and Peggy Jordan, a consultant and writer for the video *Cher Fitness* whose job it was to make sure our work followed the guidelines of the Aerobic and Fitness Association of America. They were horrified when they saw the routine, and told us, 'You can't use that! It's dangerous!' Cher and I were nonplussed. We'd been following it quite safely for over a decade! This pronouncement naturally sent everybody into a panic, including Cher, who ordered all the latest and hippest exercise people to be auditioned for her video. I went straight off and studied to get my AFAA certificate in time to be allowed to participate in the video, but it was too late and I was forced to sit on the sidelines.

From then onwards my relationship with Cher headed south, way down south. She got herself a best-selling exercise video and went back on the road, and I got to stay at home with my son. Cher and I didn't speak for many years. I didn't feel inclined to go running back to her. This silly rift only came to an end a couple of years ago, when Sonny Bono died. She reached out to me and invited me for tea; I went because part of me wanted to feel that I'd rightly ridden this one out, but mainly because I wanted to have back what I felt was part of my family. I was so happy that we were friends again. During those years of estrangement I had missed Cher and everybody around her. Cher has great presence and being around her makes me feel much better about myself.

But I didn't hang around and lick my wounds during those years away from Cher. I still wanted to teach fitness, so early in 1992 I set up another business and called it Best Bodies (Best is such a great name to have!). My years of work with Cher had certainly helped to cement my reputation, and before long I had a growing client list of celebrities who wanted me to help them look glamorous too, to get them in shape for their next film role. The business quickly built up through word of mouth, and before long I was also training the wives of Hollywood's top movers and shakers.

I worked hard at my business throughout the 1990s. I even had one client who flew me three times a week to Phoenix in Arizona just to work her out. This may sound like a tremendously glamorous lifestyle, but let me tell you, that kind of flying twice a day, three times a week for a year was exhausting. When it was over, in May 1995, I thought I'd earned myself a holiday, so I decided to go to London for a month while Calum was over there during his summer holidays. I packed all my best stuff, as we girls tend to do, and for the first week went to stay with Mary Shatila, one of George's ex-girlfriends with whom I got on really well. I was having a really great time with Mary when I started to feel rather ill. Unbeknown to me at the time, I had pneumonia again.

For my second week I had planned to stay with an American girlfriend of mine, in Fulham. So when the time came my car pulled up to this big house in Fulham and bag after bag was taken into the house by the driver and put in the hallway. I immediately told my friend I was feeling as sick as a dog and wanted to lie down. About three hours later I woke up and went down to the hallway to get my bags, but they were gone. Everything I owned, except the clothes I had been sleeping in, was stolen. Wallet, chequebook, credit cards, driver's licence, passports, plane tickets, money, keys, jewellery, all the clothes, coats, shoes and boots I had acquired over the past ten years. The police told me later that there was a gang of Moroccans cruising Fulham and the King's Road area doing robberies like this, and they suspected them. Imagining other people wearing my clothes and jewellery and reading my filofax made me cringe.

So I had nothing left but the clothes I was standing in, but once again it proved to be one of those moments in my life when His Lordship came through for me. Calum and I had to go to immigration to get new passports, and I enlisted George's help. First of all we all trooped off to the pub for a few drinks. Usually I would never have been anywhere near a pub with His Lordship, but I knew from experience that there would be a small window of opportunity after a couple of drinks where he would be in a good mood. After a few hours the three of us left to go to the immigration office, and there my plan worked. Everyone in the office was so delighted at meeting George Best and having autographs signed that they practically issued us with new passports on the spot. Seeing His Lordship standing there in his element, smiling and chatting to those people, made me realise that things would never change for him. I knew then that no matter how old or drunk he got, people would always want to shake his hand so they could tell their friends that they had met the one and only George Best.

I've always preferred the relative anonymity of living in America, but our ties with His Lordship have always seemed to work to my, and especially Calum's, benefit. There were many disadvantages to a life with George Best, but this one was a distinct advantage, and I'll always be grateful for it.

20 The Best is Now

'There were many occasions over the years when Calum would call me in tears because his dad was so drunk that he was incapable of looking after him, but then there were other times when just having Calum around made all the difference to George. If he took Calum out to dinner and ordered a drink and Calum gave him the eye – a look he inherited from his father, who famously used it on opposing players on the football field – George would pass on the drink.'

My life is simple and happy these days, but very full, and everything is done on my terms. There are no dramas or drunken episodes to complicate things any more; I can't even remember the last time I overindulged in the partying lifestyle. There are moments when I have a pang for a bit of craziness, but I feel now that I don't want to waste any more of my days. I have never been happier, I suppose because I'm not looking to anyone else to make me happy. If I had to live my life over again, I would probably do it the same way with, perhaps, a handful of changes: being a little more sensible when it came to saving money would be one, getting rid of the truly bad moments with His Lordship would be another. But throughout my life I have made choices from the heart, and I believe there is a guiding force that takes care of you, that everything happens for a reason, and that if I hadn't spent a lot of my time with His Lordship I wouldn't have our gorgeous son.

These days Calum is an international model working in Los Angeles, New York and Milan being photographed for the likes of *Vogue* and *Elle*. I know His Lordship is as proud of him as I am (he always says so, but not out loud). We all know that George, as well as being a not always adequate husband, has not exactly been the model father, and there have been times when his behaviour with regard to Calum has infuriated me. For instance, when Calum travelled to the UK to spend his summers with his dad, the only thing it seemed His Lordship ever did with him, the only way Calum could get to hang out with his dad, was to take him down to the pub. Of course, Calum loved to spend time with his dad wherever it was, and even as a child Calum would keep an eye on his father and reprimand him if he drank too much. But despite this, I always knew how much George cared for him.

There were many occasions over the years when Calum would call me in tears because his dad was so drunk that he was incapable of looking after him, but then there were other times when just having Calum around made all the difference to George. If he took Calum out to dinner and ordered a drink and Calum gave him the eye – a look he inherited from his father, who famously used it on opposing players on the football field – George would pass on the drink. I was always pleased when I heard stories about George responding to the need to be a responsible father, even though those times were few and far between.

I don't have a relationship with George these days. Firstly, he never answers the phone, and I could die a slow and painful death waiting for him to call me – which is fine really because we've grown apart and don't have a great deal in common any more. Calum is now a young, independent man and George has his new wife Alex who, when I speak to her on the phone, sometimes tells me how frustrated she is with George, how she always badgers him about calling Calum, which he very rarely does. The fact that father and son do not now have much of a relationship to speak of is not Calum's fault. I sometimes wonder what George thinks about this situation now. He just doesn't know what he is missing by letting his relationship with his son slip away. George should be getting together with Calum as much as possible, sitting him down and telling him, 'You're all I've got, son, so let's really get to know each other before I die. Let's talk.' My take on it is that Calum genuinely feels that it's his dad who needs to try harder and reach out, very much in the way Calum did for a great many years. Sometimes it is not enough to be satisfied with the thought that you know your child knows you love him.

Poor Alex is stuck in the middle of all this. She has the life she wants, but I think when she married George she was a little too young to realise the true nature of the responsibility of also taking on a stepson. As much as they say the right things, they need a practical guide to doing the right thing. Having said that, I know how stressful life can be for Alex. She is still a young woman and does not want to give up her life in London in favour of a more solitary life on the Irish coast, where they now live, but George needs her.

I want always to be there if either George or Alex needs me. In fact, just five years ago I came back to London when George was being sued by his former manager who had claimed that George didn't own the flat he lived in and that after nearly eight years His Lordship hadn't paid the mortgage. Now I know better than anyone that when George is drinking he leaves the responsibilities of day-to-day life to everyone else, but after all, that was the manager's job – to manage him. I sat powerless in the courtroom while this man took everything from George. He even got the rights to use the name George Best Management, which I had wanted to keep for Calum's use. How dare he take my son's family name away from him? I was so angry.

But then George's drinking was almost certain to rebound on him in some way sooner or later. I don't envy Alex having to look after him now. I did more than my fair share while I was with His Lordship, but in those days he was fitter and healthier and still playing football, whereas Alex has the horrible task of trying to keep an eye on an older, much more unwell George. I talk to Alex as often as I can, and when in the summer of 2000 His Lordship was taken seriously ill she called me for advice, as she often did, especially when George was playing up. I always seemed to be the first person everyone called when George was being George, but I didn't mind. When George was taken into hospital that summer, within hours of the story breaking in London the newspapers were on the phone to me asking how I felt about it all. Well, of course I was very sad when I heard about how ill George was. He was on the front pages of every newspaper again when the doctors told him he needed a new liver, that his life would probably end if he had just one more drink. I called him while he was in the hospital and for once George didn't sound like his old self. After a bender, he would usually retain that cheeky attitude of his, but this time he sounded so tired and weary and I felt so sad for him. Despite all we went through, it still hurts me when anything bad happens to George.

Calum was in Italy modelling when his father went into hospital, but as soon as the assignment finished he went to England for a few days. He went to see George and Alex (George had been released from hospital by this time), but when he got to their house in Chelsea they were not at home. Calum sat on the steps to the house and waited for them. He got the shock of his life when his dad eventually came walking round the corner. Calum said his father didn't look him in the eye and didn't hug him, which was unusual, and it was a very weird experience for him. George seemed embarrassed to see his own son, although Calum said that you only had to take one look at him to realise he wasn't at all well. He said he appeared very small, very thin and very yellow.

If Calum was shocked by his appearance, I'm glad I didn't see him. I hold in my mind's eye an image of George Best as a gorgeous young man, with long black hair, Paul Newman blue eyes and a dimple in his chin, the naughty little boy I fell in love with. In my last days with him and after I left him, this image changed into one of a seedy, gambling, shuffling drunk, a lifestyle which led to what he is today: an ill, old alcoholic in need of a new liver. But I still believe he'll pull through, in his own way, because deep down he is such a wonderful man. I desperately want George to be as contented as I am.

I now live permanently 5,000 miles away in Malibu with my eight dogs. I didn't start out with the intention of having eight dogs, but we have an animal rescue woman in Malibu called Sherman who has a store called

Sherman's Place. Every time I went in to see Sherman, who is a character beyond compare, there would be a gorgeous little puppy in need of a loving home – and who better than me to look after this poor wretch? I'm a slave to a permanent Florence Nightingale syndrome! The same thing happened with my horses. My friend Gabrielle runs a non-profit organisation called the American Foundation Against Cruelty to Equines. She called me one day and said, 'Your horse is here.' I said, 'I beg your pardon?' And she explained that she had found me a magnificent horse and that I should go over and see him. Of course I fell in love with Mr Pablo, a seventeen-hands, eight-year-old ex-racehorse, the moment I saw him. Then Harry Schwartz, Malibu's very own celebrity chef, stopped me one day and told me *he* had a horse that he didn't know what to do with because he had to move – would I take him? So I inherited Sheriff, a lovely black thoroughbred.

So I have my dogs and my horses, my needlepoint, I make necklaces, I train my girls, I work out and I write books. It's a pretty full life, but I couldn't cope with it all were it not for the fact that I have an equally insane man doing it with me. I share a beautiful home in the hills with a wonderful man called Mark, whom I met five years ago in Malibu. He had no idea who George Best was when we first got together (although of course he has learnt all about him over the years), which I found quite refreshing. All the guys I had dated in England were either famous themselves or knew exactly who I was, but with Mark I can just be myself and he loves me for that. It has taken a long time, but I finally feel I have reached a time and place in my life where I can be permanently happy. For most of my life I spent my time trying to make other people happy, or trying to do the right thing. But I have learned that no matter how hard you try, it doesn't mean anything unless you are happy too.

My business is still booming and I still work out with clients every day. Cher and I have started our fitness routine again, although it's not as fast and furious as it used to be. We both have bad backs and not quite the stamina we used to have, but the banter that goes with the workouts is still there and it's as if we haven't missed a day of those long years apart. I'm so glad that we're talking now. Cher was always someone I felt I could turn to in a crisis, which is so important in life, and she helped me out so many times when I had problems with George. And there were quite a few.

After everything I went through with His Lordship, I know George better than he knows himself, even if he doesn't acknowledge that. George may have been the drinker in the relationship, but I feel like I am the survivor. I get dozens of letters every week from women in Britain who have been through or are going through a similar situation. Most of the time they just want to share their experiences with someone, and I am flattered that they feel I am approachable enough, that they choose to share their grief and confusion with me. Others just want advice on their relationships, or their health. I try to help them all as much as I can.

I try to explain to 'my girls', as I call my correspondents, that we are only human and that we all make mistakes. What really counts is learning from them. I know I have, and I still hope that some day George will too. I tell my girls that of course alcohol affects everyone in the family, but whether you are the drinker or the partner there is *always* a way to conquer it.

Index